"What a delight! A menagerie, a bestiary, a swarm of critters all created by the Holy One and who in turn pray, weasel, whine, wax eloquent, whisper with humble awe and who could put many of us to shame in their blunt honesty and transparent worship and need of God. The book is a collection of creature's prayers in verse form—some startling, some wondrous, some hilarious and some wrenchingly sad. Each prayer is accompanied by a short pithy description of the creature and this piece is followed by a praxis for the day—a bit of theologizing and a pragmatic suggestion for incorporating this beastie's insight into your daily liturgy and life. From Anemone (not the flower) to bookworm, through Hugh Manatee all the way to Zen Xenopus there is wisdom, penetrating insight, humor and above all, gratitude and plain awe at everything that God has fashioned in their play.

"This is a book to dip into, dive into, tread water in and skim, depending on your time and feelings, experience and need, but everyone will stumble upon something that will trip them up, teach them appreciation and alter their view of creation—in other words everyone will get a sideways glance at God and an experience of contemplation that will make you laugh out loud, stop your mind, catch your breath or reduce you to tears. This book is a gift, for keeping for yourself and giving away to a dozen of your friends, to ponder, to stir your own creativity and imagination and to put new soul into your own feeble and fuzzy prayer. It says underneath it all . . . pray always, pray ceaselessly and be preyed upon . . . praying is the nature of all that is made. Bill Cleary's collection reveals that he has long been a disciple of the universe, from mite to macro and nothing has escaped his loving eye. Even the bedbugs, creeps (cobras) and rat fleas are sources of revelation—no mean feat! Cleary's critters will definitely be waiting to welcome him and all of us into the kingdom coming in glory . . . in the meantime they prove to be grand companions sharing this sanctuary called earth."

—**Megan McKenna**, author, *Blessings and Woes: The Beatitudes and the Sermon on the Plain in the Gospel of Luke* and *Keepers of the Story: Oral Tradition in Religion*

"What a wonderful, lighthearted way to teach not only prayer, but the whole spiritual life. Yet this is no lightweight book. Its depth and balance reveal the heart and mind of a veteran of the spiritual journey. A rich resource for daily reflection and prayer, it would also make a great follow-up to a retreat."

— **Kathleen Fischer** and **Thomas Hart**, authors

"In *How the Wild Things Pray* William Cleary has given us an imaginative and creation-centered psalter; the deepest longings of the heart are mediated through the wisdom of birds, beasts, insects and fish. Through the lyrical language of poetry, music and prose we pay attention to the wild and return refreshed!
"An enjoyable and enchanting book!"

— **Jim Conlon**, author, *Ponderings from the Precipice, Lyrics for Re-Creation* and *Earth Story, Sacred Story*

"This book is a joyful experience: humorous and holy, watchful and wise. William Cleary invites us to get inside the "wild things" and speak to God as they might speak. Through creative exercises he leads us in imaginative and unique ways to examine our own lives with honesty and truth — and to discover our own wild-heart. You will meet new animals and gain new insights into some of our furry, sleek, and feathered friends. An absolute delight! "

— **Macrina Wiederkehr, OSB**, author, *Gold in Your Memories*

"This delightful and insightful work of Bill Cleary is a testament to his creative imagination, his deep caring for all of creation and his hope that we humans can learn lasting lessons from our tiny, winged and four-footed sisters and brothers. To explore and reflect on our own life's journey *through* the eyes and ears of these often ignored members of our Earth community is the special gift of *How the Wild Things Pray*. Read on and enjoy."

— **Jane Blewett**, director, *Earth Community*, Laurel, MD

"According to a Sunday liturgical prayer, said in a multitude of Churches, 'All creation rightly gives God praise.' Nice words — 'But really? Skunks and alligators, fleas and elephants? Not really!' Yes, they do praise God and we can praise with them! So suggests Bill Cleary in his delightful new book *How the Wild Things Pray*. Furthermore, all God's creatures will speak to us too if we have a praying heart that listens.

"Cleary's work is a prayerbook with a sense of humor, a spiritual and whimsical journal that enables prayer in unexplored spiritual corners and discovers the presence of God in the wonders of creation. This book is a lovely 'stew,' or should we say 'zoo,' of reflections and insights into the animal world. It contains quotes from a variety of wisdom seekers. There are even songs interspersed to join the human voice to the chorus of creation.

"This book is a must for spiritual seekers — a safari into new and unexplored pathways of prayer."

— **William Fitzgerald**, author, *A Contemporary Celtic Prayer Book* and *One Hundred Cranes*

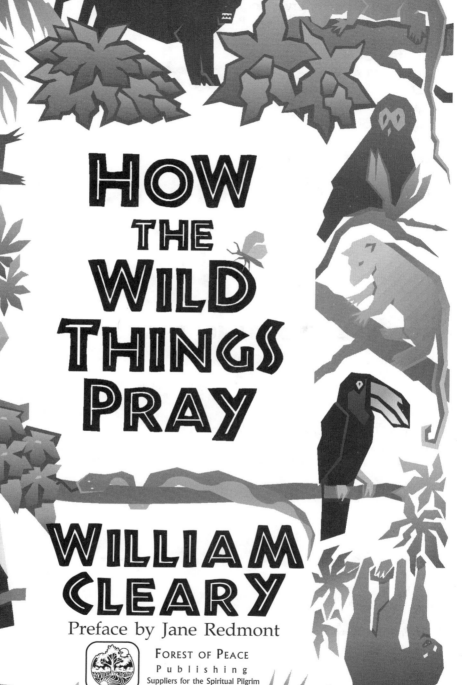

HOW THE WILD THINGS PRAY

WILLIAM CLEARY

Preface by Jane Redmont

FOREST OF PEACE
Publishing
Suppliers for the Spiritual Pilgrim
Leavenworth, KS

Other Books by William Cleary:

The Lively Garden Prayer Book
  (available from Forest of Peace Publishing)
Prayers and Fables
Prayers for Lovers
Centering Prayers
A Doubter's Prayerbook
Lighten Your Heart
Prayers to She Who Is
Churchmouse Tales from the Vatican
Psalm Services for Group Prayer
Psalm Services for Church Meetings
Hyphenated Priests
Facing God

HOW THE WILD THINGS PRAY

copyright © 1999, by William Cleary

Library of Congress Cataloging-in-Publication Data

Cleary, William
    How the wild things pray / William Cleary ; preface by Jane Redmont.
      p.   cm.
    ISBN 0-939516-45-4 (pbk.)
    1. Meditations. 2. Prayers. 3. Animals—Religious aspects—Christianity.
    I. Title.
    BV4832.2.C543   1999
    242—dc21   99-20591
                                                                CIP

published by
Forest of Peace Publishing, Inc.
PO Box 269
Leavenworth, KS 66048-0269   USA
1-800-659-3227

printed by
Hall Commercial Printing
Topeka, KS 66608-0007

1st printing: March 1999

Dedicated

to the memory
of
Vince O'Flaherty
a true blue friend

Contents

Divisions

I. Become a Disciple of the Birds . . .

Ask the animals and they shall be your teachers;
become a disciple of the birds and they shall instruct you.

—Job 12: 7

II. The Wild Beasts Will Honor Me . . .

Yes, I am making a road in the wilderness,
paths in the wilds.
The wild beasts will honor me,
jackals and ostriches,
because I am putting water in the wilderness,
rivers in the wild to give my beloved people drink.
The people I have formed for myself
will sing my praises.

—Isaiah 43: 19-21

III. Even the Smallest Ant . . .

One should pay attention to even the smallest crawling creature, for these too may have a valuable lesson to teach us, and even the smallest ant may wish to communicate with man.

—Black Elk

IV. Almost All Animals Speak . . .

Almost all animals speak. They speak in codes that we do not understand at first. They speak about danger and mates and young. They speak of life and death, of life coming out of life. Much of their passion is embedded in these signals that they send out to the world. With all our intelligence we hear these signals and strain to decipher the codes. We live in a world of messengers that we have only begun to hear.

—Joseph Mortenson in *Whale Songs and Wasp Maps*

V. Both Ancestors and Companions . . .

The animals on this earth are both our ancestors and our companions.

—Lawrence Binder in *Earth Prayers*

Preface

How can you not delight in a friend who sends you a poem about a squash — yes, the vegetable — especially when the poem is also a prayer? Now there, I thought, is a help to my spiritual life. I tacked it onto the kitchen bulletin board, and there it took up residence.

Before and since then, I have enjoyed Cleary's prayer-poems on chickens and zebras, horseradish and marigold. His inchworm prayer graces one of my own books. Cleary the Vermonter is a lover of nature, ever alert to what grows and crawls and sighs and storms. Sometimes he dresses up his animals and vegetables, and they sound remarkably like us. At other times, it is they who give us a dressing-down, surprising us with lessons from the earth and its growthful mysteries.

But it is one thing to write about handsome garden plants and winsome creatures, and another to find spiritual inspiration in bugs and beasts we tend to ignore, fear, mock or forget — or in those we simply take for granted. Here, in *How the Wild Things Pray*, come the bedbugs and badgers, whales and wolves, wild birds and beasts of desert and ocean, and with them Cleary's whimsical prayers and lessons for living. Morning meditations, nighttime readings, study breaks, refreshing pauses at work, these combinations of prayer, meditation, natural history lesson and concrete spiritual exercise — Cleary's "Praxis for Today" — are treasures and treats. Savor them. Make them yours. And, like Bill Cleary, praise the One who made these critters and made us, and who renews and sustains us all in the everyday.

Jane Redmont
author, *When in Doubt, Sing: Prayer in Daily Life*

Introduction

Like many other people, I have decided that the world around us is just too much.

Too much life. Too much mystery. Too much meaning ricocheting off the granite slopes of absurdity and up from the darkened mines of pain.

Too much of everything.

Too much distance in the cosmos. Too much speed in the arching light of dawn. Too much darkness in the unthinkable depths of every atom — in which we have now identified over 100 distinct subatomic entities, some of which, from their infinitesimal space, can trigger an explosion capable of burning up the planet we live on. Too much!

Even within the circle of earth's living things, again, it's too much. Step on the earth and your foot presses down on over a thousand living creatures. According to a recent scientific study, in a square foot of ordinary topsoil an inch deep, there lurks "an average of 1,356 living creatures ... including 865 mites, 265 springtail insects, 22 millipedes, 19 beetles and varying numbers of some 12 other forms of life ... not to mention the microscopic population that would include up to 2 billion bacteria and millions of fungi, protozoa, and algae ...."

Creation has more wonders per square foot than our brain could comprehend in a lifetime. For instance: Can anyone or anything (except light) travel as fast as 900,000 miles an hour? Answer: You! You, all of us, are moving at that speed as you read this sentence. Add together all the spins, circlings, wobbles, revolutions, rotations, loops and spirals our earth and galaxy take us through, and it adds up to 900,000 miles an hour, an incomprehensible marvel involved in just being an earthling. Much too much.

This book focuses on earthen wonders too and particularly the wonders of Wild Things — which are also "too much." Scientifically, the forty Wild Things in this book are astonishing — and symbolically their equally astonishing meaning is waiting to be discovered. Emerson said that "every natural fact is a symbol of some spiritual fact," and Victor Hugo claimed the world's animals were "nothing but the forms of our virtues and vices wandering before our eyes ... visible phantoms of our own soul." It was in that light that my creative work began.

I started out listening to the animals speak to God, and from that was able to cautiously guess at the moral lessons which, according to poet John Ciardi, are waiting to be identified in each animal.

We all have identified the overly eager beaver, the haughty rooster, the wily fox — all discernible in their prayers in this book. But did you know the whale feels plump? that the owl very much doubts her supposed wisdom? that the jellyfish and the eel are inclined to a low self-image?

Or, on the positive side, are you ready to learn how the rat flea feels awesome personal power? how the bedbug feels a worldwide medical calling? how the hen has decided that the Virgin Mary should be God Herself?

Note: Once all these animals turn to God in prayer, they soon find that the Spirit of Wisdom has taught them something — and by listening to "How the Wild Things Pray," we can share in that wisdom, and even try spiritual practices based on it. We are soon "paying attention to even the smallest crawling creature" with Black Elk and becoming "a disciple of the birds" like Job — who also found himself "brother to lizards and a companion to owls." Still, at times, alas, animals (like the Ibex — page 84 — or the Cardinal — page 28) can be as misguided as humans.

Of course, strictly speaking, the "meaning" of any living thing is not distinct from its very self and its place in the web of life, of which humans are probably only a temporary part. We have learned — especially from women theologians like Katherine Zappone — that relationship, not self, is the basic unit of spirituality, that holiness is not about individual perfection: It's about compassion, and the longing to achieve communal justice for all. Still, the analogical imagination likes to swim in symbolism, and even an ecological theologian like Dairmuid O'Murchu notes that with each living species lost through human destruction of animal habitat, "we diminish the vocabulary of our own unconscious." That's the vocabulary this book tries to call up. See if it speaks to you.

In each "Praxis for Today" you will find an element of the "offbeat" — *Laugh at Your Religion, Practice Shocking People, Read the Bible Sideways*. That's not because the wisdom that comes from the animal kingdom is cockeyed in itself, but rather because humans are often brought up on stately and pretentious rhythms like the National Anthem rather than the truer human beats of jazz, ragtime and blues.

The world's non-human critters follow a different drummer, I have found. Their prayers (if you accept my imaginings) tend to be deeper than ours in their trust, more honest in their doubts and more buoyant in their perspectives. Not a bad rhythm for human critters to learn to dance to.

William Cleary

Spring 1999

P.S. When this book was almost finished, I reached out to family and friends to help me smooth out the rough spots. To my rescue came my insightful partner Roddy O'Neil Cleary, dear friends Paul Carling and Melinda Lee, and shoestring relative John Stinchfield. If you find some questionable stuff in this mystical bestiary, it is only because I did not always follow their advice as I might have. Brought up as a hard-horn ibex, it was not always easy to be as jellyfishy as perhaps I should have been.

A Sky Hawk's Halleluia

A Mourning Dove's Coup

An Owl's Inquiry

A Penguin's Penitence

The Boo-Hoo of a Booby

Little Hen's "Hail Mary"

The Rooster's Rosary

A Cardinal's Princely Plea

1.
Become a Disciple of the Birds . . .

Ask the animals and they shall be your teachers;
become a disciple of the birds and they shall instruct you.

—Job 12: 7

A Sky Hawk's Halleluia

-≫≫-≪≪-≫≫-≪≪-

A new perspective changes everything

-≫≫-≪≪-≫≫-≪≪-

Looking down from high above,
Motionless to those below,
My heart leaps with thanks for Love
That creates the winds that blow —

Thanks for stunts we hawks can do,
Gliding on from height to height!
Looking up, you'd have no clue
What's the secret of our flight:
 How the shoulders of our wings
 Ride the wind with constant swings,
 How each wing tip "feels the air"
 With ten plumes rotating there.
 Each plume makes a figure eight
 Holding hawks high, still — and straight.

With our hawk eyes' steady stare
We rejoice at all we spy
Growing wise and more aware
As higher still we choose to fly,
 Always safe within your care,
 Children of the Wind on high.

 FOOTNOTE — Teach Us to Prey

The hawk shares many family traits with shoestring relatives like eagles, falcons, kites and vultures. The female hawk (larger, stronger and bolder than the male, and appreciably more intelligent) cares for and educates the young, while the male loves to be out hunting with his pals. A hawk's vision is eight times as sharp as that of humans, giving them a broad and enviable perspective. Hawks hunting for food glide motionlessly on wind currents, then pounce dramatically on their prey with lightning speed.

Praxis for Today:

Try a Higher Perspective

We are all perched high in a family tree. Look back down the family tree from which you branched forth.

Think of your mother and father. If they could look back down the tree, both of them would also see a father and mother from which they came. These four grandparents each look back on two more parents, and we would be well back into the 1800s.

This "looking back" perspective tells us who we are: Our forebears "locate" us, point to us, identify us. We did not emerge from the forehead of Zeus but sprouted and grew on a family tree, a tree rooted . . . where? Knowing where we came from tells us who we are. How many years back does our family go?

Scientists now can trace human mitochondria molecules — found in fossilized human remains — back 120,000 years, not just jumping back the 2000 years of our current era, not just twice that far and into the times called "prehistoric," not just ten times further than that to the last Ice Age, 40,000 years ago (which your relatives lived through). No, three times that far! Though our race may be much older than this, the fossils show evidence of our human ancestors in central Africa 120,000 years ago, and humans were there long before that.

How did the migrations start?

From Mother Africa our family members first spread north to the Middle East, then across southern Asia, crossing the Alaskan Ice Bridge into Canada, then over some thousands of years south into America, Central America, and finally — after 50,000 years — down to the bottom of South America. Meanwhile, those Middle East ancestors migrated across the Carpathian Mountains into Europe and Scandinavia, while another migration proceeded across northern Siberia and down into Japan, then China, India and all of south Asia. It all started in Africa.

So it can be said of all humans: Trace your own family tree far enough, and you will eventually come to the motherland of us all. From that perspective, one can recognize that we humans are all one family, we are all of one tree, and we all ultimately have African grandparents. You are a cousin to everyone else on earth, to everyone of any color, to everyone who has ever lived and to all future humans. They're all "family," and our only true motherland is Africa.

Does that not give you a higher perspective on who you are? Look at people on this day as if they were all cousins of yours, especially people of a darker hue, for that was our original family complexion.

God's gifts put our best dreams to shame.

—**Elizabeth Barrett Browning**

HAWK

A Mourning Dove's Coup

➤➤⫷⫷-➤➤⫷⫷

Often only music can express our deepest human feelings

➤➤⫷⫷-➤➤⫷⫷

If you hear me in the morning and think: "There's the Morning Dove!"
    You've erred: That's not the spelling of my name.
Instead my call is mournful, since I mourn from dawn to dusk
    This world's disgrace, heartache, despair and shame.

But that's my coup! my "brilliantly accomplished stratagem":
    That out of this dark world a song can start,
My mourning coo can soften all the edges of despair,
    And turn the night to morning in your heart.

A Mourning Dove I be, small, grayish-brown with spotted tail,
    A tiny dash of pink beneath my chin,
And though I mourn, I coo a song of courage through the pain,
    To bravely never-mind what might have been.

Good God, beneath the mystery of sorrow and despair,
    We also hear a clear creative call.
So doves accept the role of making music out of pain,
    Yet adding tones of hope beneath it all.

 FOOTNOTE — Peace-Loving Vegetarians

The dove is physically similar to a pigeon but decidedly more petite. All the main family groups — rock doves, turtledoves and mourning doves — live throughout the world and are strict vegetarians, preferring a disciplined diet of healthful nuts, grains and fruits. The rock dove — which often nests in rocky places — is known for its loud strident songs (divided broadly into hard rock and soft rock), while turtledoves are very shy and are seldom even seen — never in the company of turtles. The mourning dove is named for the sad cooing sound made by the male as it sings plaintively of its lovelorn life.

Praxis for Today:

Mourn with Those in Pain

There is no way for humans, however philosophical, to make pain painless.

We just must live with it. And many of us know we will probably die with it. What is asked of us is to carry on, to have hope that we can find some earthly joy despite the inevitable pain.

All attempts to grasp the intelligibility of pain, the full meaning and explanation of pain, have failed. The ancient Hebrews explained it as God's anger, but they imagined God as a domineering and distant Lord-like figure that is more misleading than enlightening. Some ancient Christians explained that the pains of their messiah — and also the sufferings of all people who "filled up what is wanting" to his pains — pacified an offended "father in heaven" who demanded "satisfaction" for sins, which made God look unfair and cruel.

Still, we grope in the darkness for some slightest measure of understanding of the meaning of pain.

Try these conventional answers in your meditations today:

Why pain?

> So there might be great pleasure and joy — in contrast?
> So there might be awe — and faith-filled resignation?
> So there might be good anger-driven imagination?
> So there might be wise humility even in times of triumph?
> So there might always be listening? and waiting for God?
> So there might exist on earth mystery impenetrable?

Why pain?

No answer is adequate.

Following the wisdom of the Book of Job, we put our hand over our mouth. Or we might groan, or chant a lament, or sing like the mourning dove.

And such music says: "Pain is our life, alas. There is nothing that can be done — but wait. The clock is ticking; time is in God's hands, and in God's plans. Our future is joy. Our present is mystery."

Job had it right. We put our hand over our mouth — so we will not murmur, but somehow, dove-like, make a melody of our mourning.

We could never learn to be brave and patient if there were only joy in the world.

> —Helen Keller

DOVE

An Owl's Inquiry

⭾⭾⭾

Wisdom requires much more than doubting and questioning

⭾⭾⭾

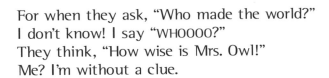

I have a query, Holy God
Who dwells above the skies:
Is it because I'm questioning
Folks think that I am wise?

The books all say I'm smart and deep
And got good grades in school,
But it's more true that I'm confused
And feel like a fool.

For when they ask, "Who made the world?"
I don't know! I say "WHOOOO?"
They think, "How wise is Mrs. Owl!"
Me? I'm without a clue.

They ask, "Who made the stars and moon?"
I say, "I give up! WHOOOO?"
Again they praise my awesome brain!
(Great Spirit, was it you?)

Tell me, Elusive Deity,
Shall someday I see you?
And learn at last your precious name,
And cease from asking WHOOOO?

 FOOTNOTE – Distinctive, Forward-Directed Eyes

The owl stands out from other birds by reason of its large, quick-moving head and shrewd, forward-directed eyes. (Most birds peer at you with just one eye at a time.) The owl's hearing is about as sharp as is humans but is much better directionally, and, once alerted, an owl can move quickly enough to catch a bat in the air. Larger owls have a wingspan of up to 6 feet and with luck can live 60 years. The many kinds of owls have a wide variety of calls, but the wisest, it is said, make the questioning sound "whooo."

Praxis for Today:

Judge Yourself Generously

We are usually unwise when it comes to judging other people, but we are often even more foolish in judging ourselves. Why?

Why are we so hard on ourselves? Why do so many of us find it unforgivable that we should be less than heroic, less than passionate in our work, unable to equal the virtuous actions of others?

Answer: **(1)** Often our vision is impaired and **(2)** Our imagination may be bent out of shape. Examine your conscience: Do you have these problems? Do you struggle to keep vision and imagination alive in your life?

(1) A wise spirituality parks us solidly in the present moment, well enough qualified for all God asks of us. If we have weaknesses, we turn them into strengths by forgiving others their similar weaknesses.

Squint a little and get a clearer look at what I am picturing here.

Are we not surrounded and inhabited by the divine love? Are we not empowered right now to enjoy the presence of God and to share in God's compassionate view of everything, yes, even ourselves? Can we not turn depression and disappointment to good use instantly by surrendering to the only judgment that matters: God's?

However unsatisfactory our feelings may be at any moment, however precarious may be our life and fortunes, if we surrender to the unfathomable mystery of God, we will not be hard on ourselves. Instead, we'll congratulate ourselves just for existing. "Just to exist is holy," said Rabbi Abraham Heschel.

(2) Cultural expectations bend our imaginations out of shape. They suggest that we constantly compete with others and incessantly judge everything in moral terms. This is nonsensical and delusional.

We are, in fact, competing with no one. Accurate moral judgments are always made in the context of the parenting love of our Creator — and parents, even among earthlings, are notoriously generous and unconditional in their care for their children.

So see yourself today bathed in God's care, exempt forever from competing with anyone or depending upon some kind of achievement for your value. Our common sense requires it. Revel in the unique creation that you are. Even your misguided attempts at self-judgments in the past are forgiven. You're home free. Enjoy the truth.

No one can make you feel inferior without your consent.

— Eleanor Roosevelt

A Penguin's Penitence

※≫《←≫《←

The reasons we give for our behavior are often far from the truth

※≫《←≫《←

O God in whom we live and are,
Queen of ocean, sun and star,
Hear this humble prayerful cry
From birds who walk instead of fly.

Oh, of course, it may seem bold
To stand for months out in the cold
Or swim at speeds beyond compare
Like we were meant to do in air.

But wingless?!!! Flippers is our fate,
Just four feet tall, with waddling gait,
Odd flightless birds who roam and stroll
Around that place called the South Pole.

Yet, God, one shame we never face,
Our secret source of deep disgrace,
The fact that penguins as a whole
Have never lived at the North Pole.

All scientists have wondered why.
It's time to give a frank reply:

We're lazy! That's the simple fact!
It's tough to swim UP on the map,
So we stay south, a cozy place,
Choosing the South's more easy pace.

Dear God, forgive our apathy,
And bless this frank apology
For living here where we prefer:
Down South, the livin's easier.

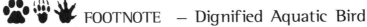 FOOTNOTE — Dignified Aquatic Bird

The penguin is a flightless but dignified aquatic bird that lives by the millions exclusively in the Antarctic. They can go for months without food and, although they breathe air, can forget to come up for as long as 90 minutes. Their muscular flippers contain all the bones needed for flying, but after a dive they use them for swimming, and sometimes live continuously in water for several months — without catching cold. Most penguins do not build nests but carry their one egg (sometimes two or — in show-off families — even three) balanced without apology on the top of their (relatively) warm feet.

Praxis for Today:

Laugh at Your Religion

Every religion seems to have some aspects that don't quite fly. Think for a moment of the amusing inconsistency between a religion based on the life and lifestyle of the humble carpenter prophet and executed criminal, Jesus of Nazareth, and the religious practices of most of his followers today.

To see this incongruity more clearly, imagine a resurrected Jesus in work jeans arriving incognito at St. Peter's Basilica for a tour that is lead by you, the tour guide.

Getting off the tour bus and peering wide-eyed at the great church from across the crowded piazza, Jesus speaks up and asks, "Exactly what is that building for?" What would you say?

Shouting and cheering begin as the pope appears on his high balcony, and Jesus asks, "Who is that exalted character up there in the tall hat? What does he do?" (See if you can answer his questions without making him laugh.)

Now totally entertained, Jesus enters the basilica with you and asks you modestly, "What is done at that great marble altar?"

A priest enters for Mass, and Jesus asks, "Why is the man dressed that way?"

As your tour leaves and heads for the Vatican Museum, Jesus asks earnestly, "Why would a messianic religion own such colossally valuable art?" (If you have no answer, at least try to look intelligently puzzled.)

His final question to you: "Which way to the nearest synagogue?"

It is the test of a good religion whether you can joke about it.
—G.K. Chesterton

The Boo-Hoo of a Booby

Coping with mistakes is a skill of immense value

We boobies won't praise you, O God,
When you deserve a hiss.
It's you designed our waddling walk,
Our sky-high dives that miss.

Though goose-sized, still like any hawk
And acting on a hunch,
We dive-bomb fish — but often end
With nothing for our lunch.

So "booby" is our given name,
And scoffs and sneers are many
As we race after flying fish
But seldom catch us any.

In love, we take high booby steps
To show how blue our toes,
While whistling males chant to the sky
And hens groan through their nose.

RIDICULOUS! That sums us up,
Our booboos never stop.
So "booby" prizes are the ones
That go to those who flop.

The one achievement that we prize
Is that we've endless ardor.
However often we should fail
We just try all the harder.

Though winning prizes is a dream
Our destinies withhold,
We've learned to smile at our mistakes!
And that's more dear than gold.

FOOTNOTE — Show Off Their Beautiful Feet

The booby is a hefty, technicolor tropical sea bird that lives by bravely diving for fish from high in the air. The instant before hitting the water, they fold up their wings and plunge deep, sometimes many of them at a time, leaving behind a prodigious splash. Boobies come in many colors and sizes, but blue-footed boobies are particularly fascinating in their mating rituals. The males walk suggestively about, occasionally holding an irresistible blue foot in the air in an ungainly high-stepping ritual that often wins the hearts of wide-eyed lady-boobies-in-waiting.

Praxis for Today:

Be Beautiful

Sometimes your day — or your year, or your life — can be saved, made meaningful, by beauty instead of by achievement, or any other measure.

Saved by beauty?

Yes.

Many religions, of course, teach the equivalent of this: that the purpose of life is "to know, love and serve God in this world and be happy with God in the next." You achieve your life's purpose through accomplishing something.

The commercial world constantly gives us its own version of this message. Money earned through work is our ideal and norm. The highly paid are the most highly honored.

This achievement norm, however, is poisonous. It can create a sense of hopelessness among those many millions who never achieve much, never earn much, never win much, never receive honors or acknowledgement or success in ordinary terms.

To these people it may be helpful to realize that there are other ways to look at the reason for being. Besides achievement, there is beauty. One of the ways to state the purpose of life is: "to be beautiful." We all know people who, quite unknown to themselves, are beautiful in their courage, in their persistence, in their ingenuity, in their patience, in their compassion and generosity, in their lightheartedness and encouragement to others. And they are particularly beautiful in the eyes of God, stunningly so.

On occasions of failure, sometimes tell yourself: "If I can't be happy today, at least I'll be beautiful. That's something." (That's everything!)

Turn your face to the sun, and the shadows fall behind you.
> **—Maori proverb**

Little Hen's "Hail Mary"

Each person has a somewhat different image of what God is like

Hail, Mary, full of grace,
The lord is *not* with thee!
He's in the castle counting eggs
Plundered all from me!

But, Holy Mary, blest you are,
    YOU ARE HENS' CHOICE FOR GOD!
The roosters name God "Mighty Lord"!
A naming I find odd —
    Were God so mighty, those he loved
    Would never be this small,
    But, Mary, God-like, you've no might —
    Except to love us all.

Blest art thou among womankind
And each created thing,
And blest the fruit of your great womb,
In which we have our being.
    Holy Mary, Mother God,
    Do pray for all us sinners,
    Or better, at the hour of death,
    Make all the least be winners.
        With your sweet femaleness on high,
        All femaleness is blessing,
        And feisty little hens like me
        Will find God less depressing.

FOOTNOTE — They Hide Their Faces

The hen is a familiar domesticated fowl that provides eggs by the hundreds of millions each year for human consumption. The common chicken always lays white eggs, in contrast to the so-called Asiatic Cochins, who prefer to lay brown eggs. Hens sometimes become quite emotional: After laying an egg, a jovial hen will usually cackle in pride; but should one lose a fight, she may hide her face for many days. Farmers know them as "short-day animals" since they retire for sleep early in the afternoon (especially if they've had an emotional day) — thus the saying, "to go to sleep with the chickens."

Praxis for Today:

Pray to She Who Is

The eminent prize-winning theologian, Elizabeth Johnson, explains this praxis in her 1992 book, *She Who Is*. She says that rather than giving God a name of some kind we are really only capable of "naming toward God," that is, using words that point toward God rather than presuming to name God.

Then, referring to the famous Exodus passage in the Latin Bible, in which the Divine Mystery utters its name as "*Qui est*," "the One who is," Johnson comments:

> Naming toward God from the perspective of women's dignity, I suggest a feminist gloss on this highly influential text. In English the "who" of *qui est* is open to inclusive interpretation, and this indicates a way to proceed. If God is not intrinsically male, if women are truly created in the image of God, if being female is an excellence, if what makes women exist as women in all difference is participation in divine being, then there is cogent reason to name toward Sophia-God, "the one who is," with implicit reference to an antecedent of the grammatically and symbolically feminine gender. "She Who Is" can be spoken as a robust, appropriate name for God. With this name we bring to bear in a female metaphor all the power carried in the ontological symbol of "absolute, relational liveliness that energizes the world."

Try it yourself today. Or use the how-to book entitled *Prayers to She Who Is*. It may become for you not just a word change, but a world change — as Johnson herself suggests. Here is a prayer from the book:

> Loving God, mothering creator,
>   She Who Is,
> lighten my heart with the sweet beauty of this life —
>   so that in my joy and my enjoyment,
> you can also know a joy for having given me birth.
> (p. 76)

God is more truly imagined than named, and more truly exists than is imagined.

— **Saint Augustine**

A Rooster's Rosary

⇒⇒⇐⇐-⇒⇒⇐⇐

More important than words of a prayer is our heart's link with God

⇒⇒⇐⇐-⇒⇒⇐⇐

Our Father, Hail Mary, Glory Be,
I pray and walk the barnyard day and night.
Our Father, Hail Mary, Glory Be,
I tell my beads and pray that all is right.

Our Father starts a Joyful Mystery;
I walk the fence and then walk back again.
Our Father, Hail Mary, Glory Be,
So God will bless young pullet, chick and hen.

Next come the Mysteries Sorrowful and Dark,
With each *Ave* I'm mourning with the Christ,
While, bishop-like, I stroll with head held high,
So dignity is never sacrificed.

As Glorious Mysteries rise within my heart,
With open beak I cock-a-doodle-do!
Declaring resurrection time for sleepers,
To rise, as from the dead, and live anew.

Our Father, Hail Mary, Glory Be,
I end my rosary in the dawning light,
One hundred-fifty "psalms" that honor Mary
And keep away the foxes of the night.

 FOOTNOTE — Defends His Hens

The rooster is a headstrong male domestic fowl, who is named for his high "roost" where he can keep a close eye on his hens, the females with whom he mates. With his all-purpose cock-a-doodle-do, he is always ready to compete for their allegiance, warn them of dangers, lead them to food and herd them back when they stray from his care. He even helps his hens find a nest where they can lay their eggs, and if a hen is dissatisfied with his first nesting suggestion, he will — with an irk-laden command — suggest another. He defends his hens and his territory with ferocious crowing and beating his wings together above his back, his sharp claws ever ready.

Praxis for Today:

Create Your Personal Rosary

Our prayerful rooster has learned to spend time with God reciting memorized prayers, a melody of praise, but with a heart connected to mystery and enmeshed with history. The fifteen traditional mysteries of the rosary (Joyful, Sorrowful and Glorious) review fascinating events in the Jesus story — but, strangely, they leave out many other events during Jesus' mortal journey.

Missing are his baptism by his cousin, his forty-day fast in the desert, the Cana wedding he attended, his "cleansing" of the temple, the murder of his cousin John, his choice of twelve apostles, the unforgettable sermons and healings, the stories of his befriending the poor, his mind-reading and marvelous deeds and, finally, the events of his Last Supper.

Each of these events may be called a "mystery" too (just as the famous fifteen are) for they have important, often hidden, significance in his life path. They are mysterious too because they contain many levels of meaning.

The same is true of each of us to some extent: Our lives are mysterious.

Look back today at the greatest mysteries of your own life: your conception, your birth, your link with each of your parents, your family experiences, each of your years in school, the individuals from whom you learned and whom you learned to love — in other words, all that has happened up to today.

Can you think of something significant about each important event? Do you detect anywhere the hand of God in your life? Invent your own melody of praise, perhaps, and enjoy a prayerful review of the joyful, sorrowful and glorious mysteries of your own rosary.

People seldom see the halting and painful steps by which even the most insignificant success is achieved.

— **Annie Sullivan**

ROOSTER

A Cardinal's Princely Plea

The path of religious leadership is invariably dangerous to the soul

I give thanks, Lord, I am not commonplace,
A common bird of plain and common face,
But rather called to heights that must be served:
To leadership, however undeserved.

My whistling prayer makes lower clergy wince
For in the church a cardinal is a prince,
Makes territorial claim, as the tiger does,
As do the sharks and skunks and walruses.

The robe I proudly wear is fiery red,
To fill all males with reverence and dread,
While females in my entourage wear brown
And keep their glimpses modestly cast down.

My plea: Lord! Top my head's red crest with gold!
To make me yet more impressive to behold
So listeners will pay heed to what I say!
With deep humility — for this I pray.

May all these prayers I place before you, then,
Not hug the earth like prayers of lowly men,
May mine instead rise up like frankincense!
Your humble servant,
    (signed) +His Eminence.

 FOOTNOTE — Dad Cares for the Young Adults

The cardinal is one of the most valiant songbirds of North America. Its call, marking its territory, is often the loudest and most insistent in the woods. While the female goes about in dull brown, the male is unapologetically bright red. Each has a crest of feathers on its head that looks like a peaked cap, the male's decidedly larger. Young cardinals leave their nest after just ten days, but the male continues to feed them while the dutiful female builds a new nest.

Praxis for Today:

Pray Humbly

Arrogance and egotism usually seep into our human lives despite all we may do to cleanse ourselves from them. Even when we turn to God to pray, it is very hard to speak honestly and humbly, and not to let isolation or egotistical desire dilute our prayer. The loftier our state in life, the harder it is to pray with humility. Understanding this, St. Augustine admitted that his role as bishop was a danger to his soul.

How can we learn to pray humbly?

One way might be to say nothing at all but simply let God read the truth about us, which is always visible in our hearts to God's penetrating wisdom. Psalm 139 is a classic of this kind of prayer. Though over 2,500 years old, it is rich in meaning, and continuously evolving, as you can see from the musical adaptation on the following pages. Its words lead us to a contemplative state where, if we follow the meaning closely, we end up in a truly humble, honest prayer.

Psalm 139

O God, your eyes have searched my soul, you've known me utterly:
> You know when I sit down and when I rise.

You know the roads I walk along; you know where I lie down;
> You know my fond delusions and disguise.

Before my thoughts become a word, you know what I will say;
> You know my past, my present, and my plans.

You lay a kind and loving hand of comfort on my head;
> You hold me, with the cosmos, in your hands.

Where will I go to hide from you, my Lover and my God?
> If I ascend the heavens you are there;

You'd find me in the house of death; you'd find me in the dawn;
> Or far at sea, you'd find me anywhere.

If I should say: "I'll hide myself in darkness and in night!"
> The darkest night is bright as day to you.

To you I turn my human face and know that you are there,
> Your presence almost too good to be true.

I try to teach my heart not to want anything it can't have.
> *— Alice Walker*

O God, Your Eyes Have Searched My Soul

say, You ___ know my past, my pre-sent, and my plans, You___
night," The ___ dark-est night is bright as day to you, To___

lay a kind and lov-ing hand of com-fort on my head, You___ hold me, with the
you I turn my hu-man face and know that you are there, Your___ Pre-sence al-most

cos-mos, in your hands.
too good to be true.

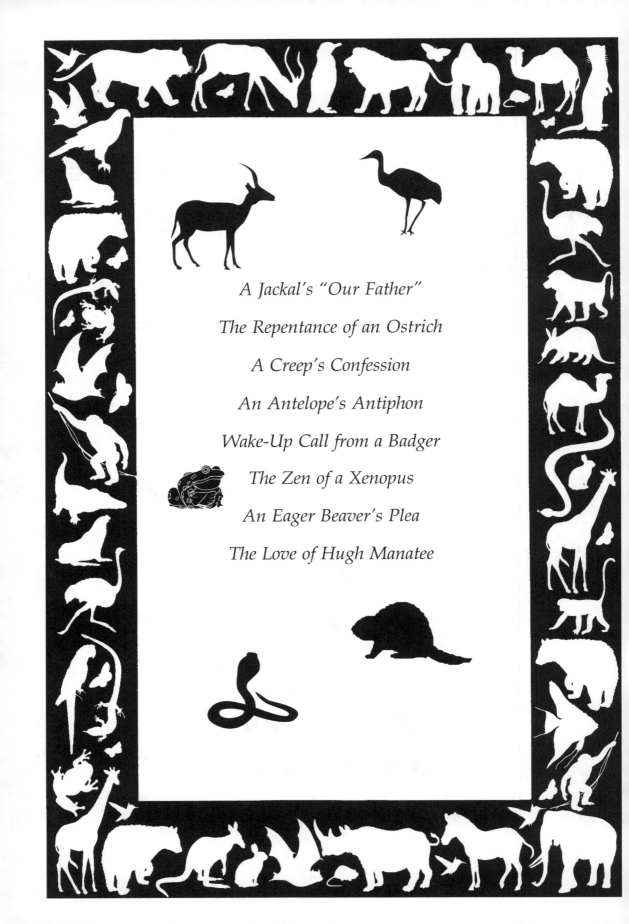

A Jackal's "Our Father"

The Repentance of an Ostrich

A Creep's Confession

An Antelope's Antiphon

Wake-Up Call from a Badger

The Zen of a Xenopus

An Eager Beaver's Plea

The Love of Hugh Manatee

11. Wild Beasts Will Honor Me . . .

Yes, I am making a road in the wilderness,
paths in the wilds.
The wild beasts will honor me,
jackals and ostriches,
because I am putting water in the wilderness,
rivers in the wild to give my beloved people drink.
The people I have formed for myself
will sing my praises.

—Isaiah 43: 19-21

A Jackal's "Our Father"

⇶⇷⇶⇷

Rejoice in your role in life even though it not be the "lead"

⇶⇷⇶⇷

Lion Father, who art in heaven,
To thee I'm just the runt
Who scares up prey for lions to eat.
So — Hallowed be thy hunt!

> Thy kingdom come, thy will be done,
> On earth — in prayer we kneel,
> Give us this day our daily bread —
> Left over from thy meal.

We jackals know we are beloved
As strong companion hounds
Who make a lion's life a joy
Wherever prey abounds.

> Alas, the human race is harsh
> In judging jackals' role,
> Unknown our faithful family life
> And how sublime our goal.

Forgive our debts as we forgive
Each lion who first dined
And always got the "lion's share":
(We get what's left behind.)

> So lead us from temptation's way,
> From evil guard our soul,
> For thine's the kingdom and the power,
> Ours — just a minor role.

But for that part, we bark you thanks
From our well-furnished den,
Where leftovers are plentiful,
Thanks to your grace. Amen.

🐾🐾🐾 FOOTNOTE — Called "The Howler"

The jackal is a much-despised, carrion-eating wild dog that acts as a faithful companion to lions, scaring up unlucky animals for the lions to prey on, and eating the remains of the kill when the lions have left. Found in Asia, Africa and even in Europe, it runs in packs and hunts mostly at night. It is often called "the howler" because of its mournful nighttime cry and unmistakable yapping. Jackals reek of a distinctive gamy smell and for that reason are considered poor pets.

Praxis for Today:

Give Thanks in Body Language

If jackals should confess gratitude to their lords, the lions, the converse is true also: Lions have much to thank jackals for.

Continual gratitude can be a natural part of human life as well. According to the Benedictine monk David Steindl-Rast, gratitude is "the heart of prayer." That's the title of his recent book.

So if we desire to live lives of prayer, we need to practice gratitude for everything we receive: for the air we breathe, for the food we are digesting, for the health of our body and the alertness of our soul and mind, for our strength to think and move, for all those we are connected to, for the past and for the future — for everything.

But this is far from easy. We are frequently distracted from giving thanks simply because life is complex, and our imaginations are busy with their own images and dreams.

So, even for one day, try praying occasionally with body language. When saying "thank you," many people place their hand on their heart: It seems natural, a gesture that can mean "thank you" by itself.

When you want to express a "thank you" to God, simply place your hand — or both hands — over your heart. God, who is present everywhere and sees all, will see your prayer and know you are grateful. You will also have the heart-touch reminder that you're engaged in the heart of prayer, the best prayer.

Keep your hand there whenever you have that prayer in your heart — and although distractions may come and go, your gesture remains and your prayer is uttered — a perfect little ritual — in body language.

Another way: the Buddhist teacher Thich Nhat Hanh suggests that one may continuously express in every moment gratitude for life through a smile on one's face. The effort it takes to achieve this is a constant reminder that our bodies speak eloquently to our creator, for God relates to us constantly.

So, the world of Spirit calls to us constantly through the world's matter, energy and relationships, and we may answer constantly if we choose in wordless body language of hand or face. Try this prayer perhaps for one day: It may be your cup of tea or it may not. Head for whatever stream floats your boat.

There is as much greatness of mind in acknowledging a good turn, as in doing it.
                                                                —Seneca

JACKAL

The Repentance of an Ostrich

A good spirituality requires not heroism but becoming one's best self

Strengthen me, Most Holy One,
To face my problems that abound
With courage and intelligence.
No cover-up! No runaround!

Alas, my poor soul hates to face
Whatever dangers frighten me.
Instead I cover up my head
Or use my mighty legs to flee.

Is it because I have the power
To run at 40 miles an hour
That I have never learned to fly
Like birds who rocket through the sky?

Why do I love to just pretend
That if I hide, my troubles end?
That this "great bird" folks think I am
Is an illusion and a sham?

O Holy One, give me the grace
Of one pure hour of honesty.
Then strengthen me as I become
The bird that I was meant to be:
Using my speed, my kick, my size,
My awkward shape, my awesome claws
To face with the brave all fearsome things,
For many a high and noble cause.

FOOTNOTE — Two Sharp-Clawed, Two-Toed Feet

The ostrich is a strange, swift-footed flightless bird — found mostly on the plains and deserts of Africa — that can grow 8-feet tall and weigh 325 pounds. Ostrich eggs are kept warm by both parents during the daytime, but baby-sitting at night is strictly the male's task, while mom is out and about with her fine-feathered friends. Though the ostrich appears benign — with a body covered with soft feathers (except for the nearly bare thighs) — its sharp-clawed, two-toed feet can be lethal to its enemies.

Praxis for Today:
Face Your Fears

We all have many fears, and usually what we fear is pain: physical pain, the pain of someone we love, failing at something, loss, ridicule, defeat, impoverishment or humiliation.

The great theologian Jurgen Moltmann once wrote that "only the willingness to suffer can overcome suffering."

Mothers tell us that the discomfort of pregnancy and the pains of childbirth are considerably mitigated because a wonderful reality — the birth of a beloved child — is in clear view. Jesus himself used this mothering phenomenon in his teaching about fear and pain: "When the child is born, a mother forgets her pain."

Under other circumstances, when a goal is not so clear, suffering can become a burden that tends to inhibit human growth of spirit. That seems natural enough.

In one sense, all of our fears are the fear of death because the pain of them diminishes us and takes away the liveliness that comes with health and serenity.

Is it possible, then, sometimes — in the case of the ordinary pains of aging and diminishment — to face the ultimacy of death as a natural part of life?

Could we not name many of our pains, and especially the aches and illnesses of aging, as "whispers from mother earth" or the Evolutionary Spirit saying: "Remember, as I am your source, so I am your destiny too; one of these days you will return your body to me, there to be useful in the evolution and growth of other life forms"? Could not other kinds of suffering and fear be brought to our consciousness as just a natural part of this temporary life?

It may be valuable to make a list of our fears and face them explicitly. It is one way to begin to grope for meaning in them.

I often remember the old man who said on his deathbed that he had a lot of trouble in his life, most of which never happened.

—Winston Churchill

A Creep's Confession

Many apparent wonders are nothing but wonderful tricks

This cobra creeps before thy face,
Great God, from my safe nighttime place,
   My basket home.
My Muslim fakir master snores,
Exhausted from his daily chores,
   And I can roam.

      A darkness animal am I,
      Awake all night, so that is why
         I snooze by day.
      And when I hear him tune his flute
      I come out dreaming, charmed and cute
         And start to sway.

            But, Holy God, I feel the need
            To now confess my phony creed:
               It's all an act!
            We both know people won't be harmed:
            I'm half-asleep, I'm hardly "charmed"!
               That is our pact.

It isn't his flute's melody!
His *swaying* hypnotizes me
   To bend and roll.
I'm seldom in a biting mood,
And never learned to chew my food.
   (I eat it whole . . .

            . . . The way my cousin pythons may:
            We first will paralyze our prey,
               Then take it in
            By just unhooking both our jaws
            To swallow it — head, tail and paws,
               Bones, meat and skin.)

So now that I've confessed my lie,
I pray we are a snake and guy
   That you'll redeem.
And any karma we have earned
Will from our souls be cleanly burned —
   Our fondest dream.

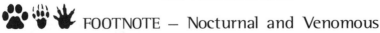 FOOTNOTE — Nocturnal and Venomous

The cobra is a feisty, nocturnal, venomous Asiatic and African snake famous for its remarkable bodily markings. When confronted with an aggressor, it stands its ground, rearing up the front of its body and expanding its hood (just below its fangs), and on the hood appear the frightening image of two large eyes and a mouth. This is the signal for enemies of every size to make themselves scarce.

Praxis for Today:

Trick Yourself into Mood Magic

Have you ever wondered why making yourself smile often makes you feel better?

This is a trick well known to many people, and even to whole cultures.

Today, when you are feeling sad or depressed, force a little smile onto your face, and sometimes your mood will change. Why this works so remarkably is mysterious, but perhaps it has something to do with the power of symbolism.

When our interior mood is genuinely upbeat, our face reflects the good mood. Often we'll smile. The smile comes to symbolize our mood. The strange truth is that this can work backwards, from the symbol to the soul. When we force ourselves to smile, an upbeat mood begins to pervade our soul.

This is different from a false smile, an attempt to deceive the people we meet. It is a true and honest smile, but just a little more deliberate than usual. Such a smile can also symbolize our gratitude for life — as was mentioned earlier.

An upbeat mantra — a simple saying repeated in our heart, like "All's well!" — can accomplish the same wonder. We trick ourselves into mood changes, and we spread joy instead of gloom wherever we go.

I feel an earnest and humble desire, and shall till I die, to increase the stock of harmless cheerfulness.

—Charles Dickens

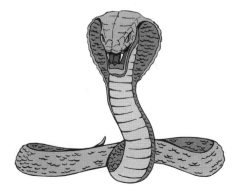

An Antelope's Antiphon

⇒»⇐⇒«⇐

If you become your unique self, you will not fit any stereotypes

⇒»⇐⇒«⇐

When I was young and full of strife,
I would complain about my life:
    How I, dear God, unlike wild boars
    Or tigers, HATED FIGHTING WARS,
Instead — in terror or caprice —
I'd run — like lightning slick with grease,
    Escape all fights — like a gazelle,
    As fast as bats fly out of hell.
I felt ashamed to be a shrimp:
In looks a stag, at heart a wimp.

Now I am old, and quite content
To simply be magnificent
    At dashing with prodigious bounds,
    Outrunning rabbits, steeds or hounds.
My famous leaps of 30 feet
Have kept my skin and bones complete,
    A streaking halfback star who glides
    Down football fields in just ten strides.
So I give thanks for what I am:
In looks a stag, at heart a lamb.

 FOOTNOTE — Some as Small as Rabbits

The antelope comes in many models, some as small as rabbits, some as sizable as cows. Most make their home in Africa. The famous Impala antelope — with hollow, back-slanted horns — is reddish-brown and capable of continuous 30-foot leaps as it gallops along to impress the opposite sex or evade a predator. It seems to prefer the achievement of grace to any confrontation or competition.

Praxis for Today:

Get a Spiritual Workout

However we may appear to others, our hearts sometimes belie our appearance. When negative feelings begin to dominate our heart's truth, we need to train ourselves in positivity.

Sometime when you are out for exercise — jogging or cycling or just on a walk — bring an antelope-lightness to your step and your heart, and add a spiritual exercise to your regime: Put on rose-colored glasses.

In other words, look at everything differently than you normally do: Make yourself see only the beautiful aspects of things. Try not to avert to the imperfections, the dangers, the regrettable or the injustices.

For a change, see only the beauty: the promise in the eyes of the youthful, the healthy drive everywhere for goodness and pleasure, the ambitious design of all the houses and buildings, the wonders of energy and magnetism at work on all sides, the sweet attraction between affectionate teenagers, the physical vitality and amazing heart muscles keeping each person alive and conscious, the life force thriving in everything that grows and moves — the grass, the trees, the birds, the bees, and then the remarkable earth itself surrounding and caring for us. For it all gives praise to God, that "relational liveliness that energizes the universe," in theologian Elizabeth Johnson's words.

It's hard at times to find much meaning in the world around us, but on this day you will. You will probably return home upbeat. And perhaps you may experience the world a little bit of the way God does.

There is no duty we so much underrate as the duty of being happy.
—Robert Louis Stevenson

ANTELOPE

Wake-Up Call from a Badger

Each soul's search for God is a little different

Dear God most high, great Mystery Deep,
I hope tonight you're not asleep
And this, our prayer, awakens you
And interrupts a dream or two.

We badgers come alive at night
And raise our faces, black and white,
To you — in prayer that we will spy
Fat grubs this night in good supply.

We sense you're deep within the ground,
A secret place that few have found,
But we will find you, soon or late:
There's nothing we can't excavate.

We're diggers extraordinaire
And love researching everywhere
To find each night our daily bread,
And then by dawn we're back in bed.

So smile, great God of earthen face,
And grant us grubs and truth and grace,
Provide our feast of things that creep,
And then you can go back to sleep.

 FOOTNOTE — Wears a Black-and-White Face Mask

The badger is a small, good-humored, fast-digging member of the weasel family (to which skunks and otters belong), usually silver and gray and about 2-feet long. Its name comes from the black and white "badge" it wears across its face. It claimed to be able to outdig any other animal on earth — until backhoes were invented.

Praxis for Today:

Seek God in Some New Way

Theologian John Sayre says, "Religion isn't yours firsthand until you doubt it right down to the ground."

If this is true — and it well may be — we need not be afraid of doubt. Rather, we should distrust anything we believe without at least an occasional reexamination.

So today exercise your brain and heart a little. Shine your questioning little flashlight into the darkest mysteries. Try "No" as the answer to these questions. Or, "Yes and No."

Does your God really exist? Does any God exist? Does only one God exist? Can we trust God? Can we speak to God?

Do those who have died still exist? Do they love us still?

Do we really know our own truest selves, the way we appear in God's eyes?

Is our spirit immortal so that we will live on somehow after death?

Are we humans part of the earth itself?

How much of what we have learned about the world around us is in fact true?

How many of those we love are as deserving of love as we think?

How benevolent is the world we live in?

Are the vast distances to planets and stars full of meaning?

Does God endorse the way we worship, what we do for work, where we live, our attitudes and connections with others?

Are we truly surrounded by God's loving wisdom and care?

Try answering each question with a "No"; then dig like a badger to dispute your own answers.

Or try doing this exercise with a companion or in a circle of people, then share answers verbally. This can be scary for some, but done in a context of friendship and acceptance, it can be wonderfully focusing. As an exercise today, doubt your religion right down to the ground — and make it thereafter yours firsthand.

If we begin with certainties, we shall end in doubts; but if we begin with doubts, and are patient in them, we shall end in certainties.

—Francis Bacon

BADGER

The Zen of a Xenopus

➜➤❮❮➜➤❮❮

Pray as you can, not as you can't

➜➤❮❮➜➤❮❮

Dear God, hear this frog
From an African bog,
As I croak out my worship and dread,
I'm without teeth or tongue
So plain words can't be sung:
I'll just slobber Zen koans instead.

I'll applaud all you've planned
With the clap of one hand
And give praise to your name with a jump.
And like trees that are downed
When nobody's around,
I'll land without making a thump.

Zen frogs all insist
One can't claim to exist,
So much less can one's praying be heard.
To catch something to eat
We can jump 40 feet —
But a leap of faith still seems absurd.

But koans, we find,
Do enlighten the mind:
We kill Buddha whenever we meet him!
So if you're a frog
From an African bog,
Though God's absent, it's still wise to greet him.

🐾 🐾 🐾 FOOTNOTE — An Ill-Mannered Leap for Food

A xenopus (ZEN-o-pus) is a name covering many kinds of African aquatic frogs that have broad triangular heads, weak forelimbs, but muscular, clawed hind limbs. Strangely, they have no tongue for snagging food but instead do ill-mannered leaps — up to 40 feet — to catch insects in the air or small fish in the water. They lack teeth as well, so they unceremoniously swallow their meals whole.

Praxis for Today:

Try a Buddhist Meditation

Our xenopus frog is practicing a Zen style of meditation wherein the focus on non-rational questions and concepts centers us in the enlightened realization that ultimate reality — God and the things of God — is beyond comprehension. There is great value in this approach to avoiding illusion and clarifying expectations.

Another meditation model recommended by more traditional Buddhists is this: to dwell on the thought of someone we decidedly care about, and after we focus on that one person, to extend our circle to several other closely loved people. Gradually we widen the circle, taking in more and more people — until we have encircled the entire world within our caring. This may be a more feminist style since, generally speaking, it is the particular gift of women to function within a web of relationships rather than to consider themselves primarily as isolated individuals.

The voices of women are finally being heard within Christianity. They have had a profound effect on modern spirituality — especially in the widening currency of the conviction that the starting point of spirituality is relationship, not the self. This means, for instance, that if there would be any way to measure or appraise human moral achievement it must be based on relationship: how a person is connected and enmeshed with others. People matter, honest conversation matters, kindness matters, love matters supremely: the warmth of the heart, the patience of forgiveness, the wisdom of listening to and telling true stories.

In years past, we have all heard of other spiritualities, those based on personal achievement, on withdrawal from ordinary life, on keeping rules or even knowing certain secret formulas of words. These are of doubtful value, though canonization and "sainthood" were sometimes based on them. We live in an age of an enriched spiritual wisdom, thanks in large measure to the long-awaited voice and experience of women.

One can endure sorrow alone, but it usually takes two to be glad.
— **Elbert Hubbard**

XENOPUS

An Eager Beaver's Plea

—>>⟨⟨—>>⟨⟨—

We must all work together to rescue our wounded earth

—>>⟨⟨—>>⟨⟨—

Good God, in stress I turn to thee,
I have my work cut out for me:
    TO SAVE THE EARTH, no more, no less than that.
The shorebirds and the waterfowl,
The mink, the moose, the ducks, the owl,
    The humans, all fear for their habitat.

They're draining wetlands left and right!
Three-fourths of them are gone from sight!
    And we're the only force against that sin.
The critter world meanwhile is fearing,
Swamps and bogs are disappearing,
    And the threat of drought is genuine.

Good God, strengthen my teeth today
That I may gnaw despair away,
    Creating beaver dams for fens and bogs,
So kits and kids of every kind
Tomorrow will good lodgings find,
    Saved by a wall of vigilance and logs.

 FOOTNOTE — A Remarkable, Scale-Covered Tail
The beaver is a furry animal, colored brown to black, weighing up to 50 pounds, and with a remarkable tail that is wide and scale-covered and acts as its paddle. While beavers often gnaw down trees to build dams and ponds, they spend a lot of their time working underwater, cleverly closing their ears and nose whenever they dive. They live in family groups of 4 to 12, inhabiting lodges that are largely underwater with entrances no enemy can find: under the surface.

Praxis for Today:

Learn Green Wisdom

Meditate awhile today on yourself as being "the thinking part of Mother Earth."

Not separate from the earth, not on earth, nor on top of the earth — you are part of the earth itself, and a particular part: the "thinking part" — in the words of geologian Thomas Berry. (You do other things than think, but thinking is your unique role, one that only you can do — and that gives you a responsibility to think about all the earth and all its parts.)

"I am the earth." Imagine it: You are not separate from Mother Earth and all her progeny but a part of each aspect of earth:

- ♦ part of the swirling, world-mothering ocean of air surrounding everything on the world's face 75 miles deep
- ♦ part of the millions of fish in the crashing oceans that cover 7/8ths of the earth
- ♦ part of the prodigious world of tens of millions of insects and birds, reptiles and mammals that populate this spinning globe from pole to pole
- ♦ part of the green-growing vegetation rising into life in response to our daystar, the sun, that warms everything to life (The sun is considered a part of the earth too.)

St. Paul asks: "Can the eye say of the hand, I have no need of you?" Similarly, can the Thinking Part say of the trees, the rivers, the worms, the grass: I have no need of you? Hardly. Mull that over today. And try to hear all the earth speaking back to you: We have great need of you!

"I think, the earth thinks." That's green wisdom. *Green* because it harmonizes you with the prevailing color of Mother Earth of which you are a part; *wisdom* because it sweetens all the information you may have about the earth. Wisdom, according to philosophers, is knowledge plus an appropriate feeling of its importance.

Be greenly thoughtful today. Be the thinking element of our great Mother Earth. That's all she asks of you.

We are the curators of life on earth, we hold it in the palm of our hand.
— **Helen Caldicott**

The Love of Hugh Manatee

➤➤❮❮➤➤❮❮

Every created thing, even the toughest, depends on love for survival

➤➤❮❮➤➤❮❮

Behold, this manatee named Hugh
Cries out in prayer, God of the Sea.
Though thickly skinned and seldom seen,
Still I'm endangered as can be.

For food I dive down deep below
And now and then come up for breath,
But oil spills can spoil the food
And boat propellers can mean death.

Who cares about my unsafe life?
Who cares about Hugh Manatee?
Sure, "Love your neighbor as yourself,"
But who says, "THAT applies to ME!"

To love my neighbor as myself
The first one I must love is me.
So I have made my lifelong quest
To learn to love Hugh Manatee.

I love my coat, gray-black and slick,
My broad, round tail that gives control.
I'm proud to be a swimming ace
Who never harms a living soul.

Be with me, God of all that is,
And hear my strong and humble plea
That human hearts throughout the world
Soon learn to love Hugh Manatee.

 FOOTNOTE — No Hind Legs

The manatee is a very bulky, good-natured, air-breathing water mammal found in many parts of the world. It is helpless on land since it has no hind legs, but it moves swiftly in water with paddle-like front legs and a strong propelling tail. A manatee can be 14-feet long and weigh up to 1,500 pounds. It lives in coastal bays and eats about 100 pounds of tossed green salad a day.

Praxis for Today:

Love Hu-manity

Make it your custom during this day to listen with special reverence — as part of your spirituality — to the words of people at the bottom of the social ladder, however you may define that: the low-paid, the invisible, the have-nots, the homeless, the servant class, the stoop labor, as well as those marginalized for any reason.

This was strikingly the practice of Jesus, who extended his particular care to "sinners," to people with leprosy, to individuals under threat of public execution and to the lowest caste of all: women. Table fellowship, where solidarity happens most naturally, was his favorite religious practice. We can do the same, at least once in awhile.

The Judeo-Christian Scriptures often recommend this, a solid indication of that tradition's authenticy as genuinely inspired by the real God.

Don't be hesitant in speaking to the "oppressed," though they may be surprised at first by your openness. Your reward for reaching out will often be hearing a wisdom you never knew before: the wisdom of patience, the beauty of courage, the strength humans are capable of, a trust almost unconditional, an enlivening spirit unquenchable by adversity or failure or isolation. Our society's outcasts are souls made for love who still reach out in faith and humility and even humor: What a wisdom that entails!

The best portion of a good person's life is the little, nameless, unremembered acts of kindness and of love.

—William Wordsworth

III.
Even the
Smallest
Ant . . .

One should pay attention to even the smallest crawling creature, for these too may have a valuable lesson to teach us, and even the smallest ant may wish to communicate with man.

—Black Elk

A Rat Flea's Tale

To survive, every living thing must believe in itself

Up from the very deepest depths
Of critter degradation,
O God of Life and Sun and Stars,
I send this proud narration.

If you look down the graded lists
Of menial creation,
Below the snakes, below the gnats,
You'll find my lowly station.

I'm just a flea who rides a rat,
Quite tiny but athletic,
Who innocently sips the blood
That keeps rats energetic.

My role in life is quite robust,
Though just a big ironic:
When I start biting human folks,
They call my bite "bubonic."

So though I'm small, my deeds are great,
And history shows my story,
Once twenty million died at once!
"The Black Death" was my glory.

So I've reversed creation's plan!
Though wee, my power's tremendous,
The last are first! The poor prevail!
And fleabites are stupendous!

So I give thanks I bring the Plague —
At least folks won't just titter
At fleas — who otherwise would be
The world's most trivial critter.

FOOTNOTE — Can Jump 13 Inches

A flea is a tiny ebullient, wingless insect that resides on birds and mammals, and occasionally makes use of its host's blood for its food. A flea has stalwart spiny legs that enable it to move quickly and easily through hair or feathers. Long distance leaping is also a flea's specialty — it can jump as high as 13 inches, 50 times its own height — which comes in handy when the flea has to move from one host to another.

Praxis for Today:

Make Upbeat Music

If any critter on earth should feel depressed, it would be the rat flea: But behold, it's a bundle of good feelings. Not a bad ideal for humans.

Each human is a musician in one sense. We all make sounds and gestures that we put together artfully to express something inside: a thought, a hurt, a joy, a response.

We may think of this as music, our own particular melody — which usually communicates something to other people or even to ourselves: often feelings or deep inner stirrings. The tenor of our voice and its pattern are part of this music, and, in fact, the look on our face carries some impact — like a drumbeat behind a song.

Most of us can think of acquaintances whose arrival is like the coming of a song, either upbeat or sorrowful. People seem to put out "vibes," vibrations that affect us non-verbally, or, you might say, musically.

The point: Musicians often choose the music they play, and we may all do so.

Even if our exchange with someone is just small talk, still we can choose to present our words in a joyful major key or a minor, sad-sounding, key. The choice is ours. Answering the phone, for instance: What key will we select?

Even when the encounter is more serious, we may choose to proceed as a good musician might: an introduction that starts where our listener is, a lyric or melody that can catch the ear of our listener, a duration that honors our listener's mood.

So be musical today: nothing too loud, too complicated, tiresome or out of hearing range. Your friends may liken an encounter with you to hearing a song, an all too rare human experience. And it may become just the natural expression of a gradually more harmonious self.

Make a little upbeat music today. Set the world dancing, if you can.

The joy of the mind is the measure of its strength.

—**Ninon de Lenclos**

A Bedbug's Blanket Blessing

Many noble professions are underappreciated

I bless my job, I bless my life,
I bless my destiny!
    My medical vocation
    Fits my temper to a tee.

I love the task of testing blood
To see if it is sweet,
    Make sure it serves your body parts,
    Especially your feet.

I come at night to taste your blood
With perfect bedside care,
And should I find you are unwell,
I add you to my prayer.

    I also check the birds and bats
    To keep them healthy too,
    So "bedbug" is no name for me!
    A "Nurse-Bug" is more true.

I never dreamed when I was young
Such grace on me would flood.
Behold! The Nurse-Bug of the World!
(God, may I check your blood?)

FOOTNOTE — The Bug Who Loveth the Darkness

The bedbug is a tiny, reddish-brown, high-minded invention of God, about 1/4 inch long. It is skilled at hiding itself and its family in the cracks and crevices of human habitations, and availing itself — at nighttime only — of the host's blood for nourishment. Though it has wings, its species has not yet learned to fly, and the bedbug has to walk wherever it wants to go, patiently dragging its useless wings around. A bedbug's life lasts only about one year, but females lay some 200 eggs at a time, and live to see about three or four batches of their beguiling baby bedbugs hatch in their lifetime.

Find Happy Friends

"Happiness," said Erasmus, "is being content with what you are."

Do you know people who are content with what they are? They are not always just the lucky and the successful. Often enough they are ordinary people, even people with serious illness, people whom fate has heavily burdened, people seemingly left out or dramatically challenged by life.

Somehow they may still have a light heart. They may always have a new joke to tell you, or they may mysteriously seem to care about your life. They may even think of you as an important part of their life — and this can be as bewildering as it is comforting.

We all know a few of these people. Occasionally — as a spiritual practice — overcome your shyness and reach out and connect to the happy-hearted. Some of them have made a life-work of their charism for humor, for making light even of their limitations. Joan Rivers once said: "No female comedienne alive today was beautiful as a young girl." Her implication: If you can't be beautiful, you need to learn to be funny. George Burns at his 100th birthday party, commenting on how busy he still was, said: "I can't die: I'm booked." His lighthearted manner helped millions of people to cope with life's heavier burdens.

On a lesser scale are those acquaintances of ours who seem able to make us laugh. Reach out to one of them today, overcoming your own shyness — as a spiritual praxis.

Call one up, or drop a line, or pay one a visit. They have been put on earth to cheer us up. Give them a chance to do so.

The profoundly wise Indian Jesuit, the late Anthony de Mello, once wrote: "The source of every human suffering is to see as permanent what is, in essence, passing." Conversely, what makes for happiness is staying aware of what is, in essence, passing. Stay lighthearted, in other words: Learn happiness from your happy — and passing — friends.

Laughter is the sun that drives winter from the human face.
                                              —Victor Hugo

An Anemone's Non-Enemies

Everyone is enviable in some ways

Dear God, is there not something wrong
About us creatures who live long,
All supercharged with youthful flame
Beyond the limits of our frame?

We undersea anemones
With virtually no enemies
Survive down on the ocean floor
For 1,500 years or more!

Each one of us a bud-like sprout,
Just tiny polyps hanging out,
Together, standing safe and tall,
Caught by the wonder of it all.

But is it right? While fish swim by
And come and go and live and die,
Anemones live on and on,
With dearest friends long dead and gone.

So give us all the life you might,
But make us humble in our plight,
When once a year our friends' hearts break
To count the candles on our cake.

FOOTNOTE – It Can Live Almost Forever

A sea anemone (an-NEM-uh-nee), the longest-living animal on earth, is a small, well-mannered creature shaped like a cylinder and topped with tentacles that reach out gently and gather food into its mouth. Bright colors give it a plant-like appearance, resembling the anemone flower. It can move about slowly, but usually remains fixed to the same rock and is content there for a thousand years or more. The anemone can reproduce in many ways: by forming eggs, by dividing in two, or by budding (where the young grow out of the base of the parent's body). It's an expert at life in no hurry to die.

Praxis for Today:

Prepare For Death

However immortal you may be feeling, spend some time today preparing for your death. It is somewhere ahead on your calendar and mine, but on just which date, of course, we can't know. Still, as surely as night follows day, death follows life. The day of our death lies ahead. Today, prepare yourself a little.

The Gospel accounts of the terrible crucifixion of Jesus record his seven "last words." Just as his strength was finally leaving him, Jesus uttered his touching prayer of surrender and hope: "Into your hands I commend my spirit."

Adding to that beautiful prayer the meditations collected by Christians and Jews over the centuries, here is song echoing the bewilderment and trust of many voices. The late, much-beloved writer Anthony de Mello proposed the following question to his disciples: "What song will you want your heart to sing when you are dying?" Think about it today. Perhaps make up your mind: which song? Below is the author's poetic mix of metaphor and rhyme for his own day of death. Its music is on the following two pages.

> Into your hands I commend my spirit, into your hands;
> Into your hands I will send my spirit, into your hands.
>> Safe will I be, sheltered with thee,
>>> Safe in your perfect care,
>> Every desire, every deep dream,
>>> Hopes for a homeland there.
> Into your life I commend my spirit, God of my heart;
> I turn my face toward the Promised city, ready to start.
>> All my past ways your graciousness show;
>> Surely ahead your presence I'll know.
> Into your hands, into your life, I go.
>
> Into your hands I commend my spirit, having no fear;
> Unto the end I can trust your spirit, your strength is near.
>> Every clear day, every dark night,
>>> I knew your love was there.
>> So in this dark shadow of death
>>> I sing a trustful prayer.
> Into your life I commend my spirit, so let it be;
> Out of my death you will take my spirit, welcoming me.
>> Life was a gift, a season to grow.
>> This is the hour of harvesting, so
> Into your hands, into your life, I go.

I look upon life as a gift from God. I did nothing to earn it. Now that the time is coming to give it back, I have no right to complain.

—Joyce Cary

ANEMONE

Into Your Hands

A Bookworm's Boast

Your work may serve many more purposes than you know

Ye gods who publish thick, dull books
By intellectuals preferred,
    Rejoice to know that there exists
    Some worms who cherish every word.

Each fussy editor of late,
Whose manuscripts we masticate,
    Should know each red mark that he tries
    Tastes just like ketchup on our fries.

So keep it up! Crank more books out,
We turn them into sauerkraut.
    We each become a master sleuth
    And find how sweet can be the truth.

Besides, we tire of Donne and Keats,
A diet much too big on sweets.
    Don't shred those books! They'll fine you flat,
    Endangering bookworms' habitat!

But if someday you gods all must
Creep unsurely toward the dust,
    Rejoice to know that unaware
    You've served "consumers" everywhere.

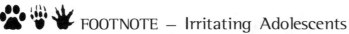 FOOTNOTE – Irritating Adolescents

The "bookworm" is a convenient name given to any number of irritating insect larvae ("adolescents") that feed on the binding and paste of books instead of using them for what they were meant for. "Larvae" are the progeny of those living things whose shape as young is very different from their adult shape, an amazing phenomenon common among insects, fish and most amphibians. Savvy adults usually rejoice that the young do not too much resemble their elders.

Praxis for Today:

Read the Bible Sideways

There is excitement and wisdom hidden in that library of delicious, ancient books we call "the Bible," but the good stuff is not always easy to find. Thick books (which bookworms especially relish), like *The Oxford Dictionary of Quotations*, make other approaches possible: either leapfrogging or reading sideways.

Leapfrogging: the Oxford Dictionary puts the Bible and all their quotes from it under "B" near the front of the book, just after "Bevin" and just before "Bickerstaffe." One can simply read down the list of quotations, leapfrogging through the pages from quotable line to quotable line, all through the fifty pages the book devotes to its biblical section. This will open up for you a smorgasbord of delicious tidbits of religious insight, passages considered quotable because they have meant a lot to the Abrahamic religions for thousands of years.

Reading sideways is even more exciting. In the Oxford Dictionary's index (in the back), under the word "joy" there are nine entries that lead you to quotations about joy here and there throughout the Bible. Under "death" there are twenty-four. Under "love" there are countless references.

This makes possible another novel approach to Bible study. There are categories that fit together — like pray, prays, prayer, praying — all leading to biblical passages. Or one can study mercy/merciful, or forgive/forgiven/forgiveness or eternal/eternity.

Of course, most biblical scholars urge us to read whole books of the Bible at a time, keeping them in context and referring to footnotes to help in understanding correctly. But an intuitive search is legitimate as well, and scholars and non-scholars alike have always enjoyed it.

The frosting on the cake is to fill in your meditation with quotations on the same subject from your favorite authors. The Oxford Dictionary has dozens of wise sayings on every biblical subject. This approach may suddenly bring the Bible to life for us, avoiding the usual lengthwise search for inspiration, which so often is unrewarding.

So, today, find a biblical dictionary of quotations, and, while sitting motionless, try biblical leapfrogging or, while remaining upright, read your Bible sideways.

Since the Gospel teaches the equality of women, no wonder the church didn't want women to preach the Gospel.

—Elizabeth Cady Stanton

BOOKWORM

The Curse of a Hermit Crab

Human contact is essential to keeping one's bearings

Begone, Wild Spirit, let us be!
We have no prayers to waste on thee.
In stolen shells, hidden, outcast,
Here we feel safe, alone at last!

How did we get so crabby? Lord,
We got this way because we're bored,
And burdened with much ridicule
Since crabs swim backwards as a rule.

It's all because we once broke free
Of orthodox society
And chose the hermit's life sublime.
Alas, we then lost track of time!

No bells or sundials or TV,
Crabs still consider it B.C.,
When ways of counting are reversed,
The higher numbers coming first.

Likewise, our clocks all backwards run
Start down from 12 and end with 1,
And counterclockwise move their hands:
Which messes up the best-laid plans.

Believe me, hermits feel like duds
When May rain brings the April buds,
And one feels pinchy, stressed and sour
When growing younger every hour.

So now you see why crabs are cursed
With always swimming fanny first:
It fits with time that's passing by
But counting backwards, who knows why?

FOOTNOTE – Walks and Swims Like No Other
The crab is a backward-swimming, sideways-walking amphibious animal covered by a hard shell, with three sets of jointed legs and large pitiless claws. There are more than 4,500 kinds of crabs, each more contrary than the other. Some crabs weigh up to 12 pounds, others are as small as a pea and live within the shells of live oysters. Others live in trees. Hermit crabs hang out in abandoned shells of other animals. Crabs are generally not very friendly and thrive on solitude.

Praxis for Today:

Find Solitude, Avoid Loneliness

Being alone, according to the spirituality classic *Gift from the Sea*, is an experience that ideally we should have a little each day, a lot each week and a generous amount each year.

Anne Morrow Lindbergh made spiritual history with the book, which has sold over a million copies since its publication in 1955. She claims she literally stumbled on this wisdom. Unavoidable circumstances first caused her aloneness, but these isolated meditations occasioned unexpected insights. Many people are terrified to be alone, but faith helps us realize that we are never really alone and that the wonder and joy of solitude is found on the other side of the fear.

Lindbergh discovered that in solitude we can learn to be good company for ourselves. And this quality makes us better company when we return to our friends. When alone, we are reminded of our one-on-one relationship with our Creator, a valuable asset at times when aloneness is unavoidable and might be otherwise frightening — including the thought of, and eventual experience of, death.

The cliche "everyone dies alone" should not really be true. Ideally our dearest friends and family will accompany us to the doorway of death, and a thousand loving acquaintances will welcome us on the other side.

So today, take a little time to be alone, and plan weekly time off and, if possible, an annual retreat in solitude — and, in that way, avoid loneliness.

Language has created the word loneliness to express the pain of being alone, and the word solitude to express the glory of being alone.

— Paul Tillich

A Mousie's Emergency
(God Steps on His Tail)

⇒⟩⟩⟨⟨⇒⟩⟩⟨⟨

Those in pain are often too shy to cry out for help

⇒⟩⟩⟨⟨⇒⟩⟩⟨⟨

Eeeeeeek!
Is there a chance, Great Czar,
You'd move from where you are?
  OUCH! Psst! O please don't take Divine Offendage!
Your more-than-ample shoes
Aren't picking up the CLUES!
  They're CRUSHING my posterior APPENDAGE!

Eeeeeeek!
You don't appear to hear…
Why was I cavalier
  To leave that tail of mine behind me showing?
Born shy and cursed with fright,
Now stuck out in plain sight
   Until… Ahhhhhhh!
   Whew!
   I'm saved! — Without your knowing!

Gods strolling everywhere!
Have you ears to hear a prayer?
  Do you know the agony shy folks go through?
When we hide our whiskered face
In a dark and secret place,
  When we tremble, God, do we get through to you?

Or are you also shy,
When you just can't satisfy
  Our daily prayers too numerous to mention?
In the future, I won't beg!
I'll just scamper up your leg
  Next time I need to get divine attention!

🐾🐾🐾 FOOTNOTE — Its Name Means "Little Thief"

The word mouse comes from an old Sanskrit word meaning "little thief" — which proves semantically that this rascal has been thieving from humankind for thousands of years. Its main means of self-defense is ducking out of sight, and it is remarkably clever at it. Your friendly female house mouse may have young about every 30 days, and female infants may have their own young when only 45 days old. So if you're into math, note that mice are superb multipliers. That's why they often end up underfoot, even in heaven.

Praxis for Today:

Comfort the Shy

Everybody is shy about something, even — according to this mouse — God.

Perhaps we are shy because there are so many embarrassing mysteries connected with us. Within, we wonder what people might think if our hearts were laid bare. On the outside, we are usually careful about how we appear — because we have often failed in our attempts to live up to what we would like to appear to be.

And we have our private secrets also. These make us shy: our remembrance of failure and pain, and our anxiety about future embarrassment. We naturally keep secret those anxieties.

Thinking about our own shyness should prepare us to be something of a comfort today to extremely shy people.

Psychologists tell us we will be comforting to shy people if we avoid looking directly at them for long, if we ask no questions, if we "let them be," if we, in fact, imitate their manner and body language. We ourselves have lots to be shy about; let our shyness meet theirs. They will find it comforting, and sometimes their response will be a model to heal us of our own shyness.

Find a shy person or persons today, and honor their shyness by reverencing their manner of being. Or be with them but without intrusive expectations. Shy people suffer from so much isolation — we don't need to add to it. We simply need to find ways to be with them on their terms at first, then gently celebrate their gifts so they won't, out of fear, contrive to hide them.

I felt a large roominess in his company, a spiritual roominess.... He didn't suffocate me with "concern."

— Eugene Peterson

An Oyster's Bedtime Prayer

Surrendering to sleep can be an act of profound trust in God

Now I lay me down to sleep,
My oyster bed is soft and deep
   Beneath the ocean's roar.
Before I drift into a dream
In glowing luxury supreme,
   I pray and I adore.

I pray the night prayers of an oyster,
Much more snug in my moist cloister
   Than pious nuns of yore.
Here humbly I produce a mere
Five hundred million eggs a year:
   I wish I could do more.

And I adore creation's twirls,
Where irritations turn to pearls
   Within my sacred space.
Although I haven't eyes to see,
Behold, mere grains of sand can be
   Occasions of your grace.

If I should die before I wake,
I pray, dear God, my soul you'll take
   To heaven's clammy foam,
Where I can peek out of my shell
And see rich shoals where I can dwell
   Forever safe at home.

FOOTNOTE — Its Skeleton Surrounds It

The oyster is a good-natured sea animal with a soft body inside a hard two-piece shell that is actually the animal's skeleton surrounding it. This skeleton consists of two concave panels decorated on the inside with mother-of-pearl, and connected by an ingenious hinge — which the oyster slowly opens when it is hungry or mate-hunting. The dazzling white pearls produced accidentally within oyster shells are some of the world's most valued gems. The oyster's only natural enemies are humans (who have eaten them for thousands of years) and sharp-beaked sea birds, who know how to pry their shells open or crack them open by dropping them on rocks.

Praxis for Today:

Grow a Pearl

Some night soon as you settle down in bed, take a lesson from your oyster siblings. Think of some irritation within the shell of your inmost self — perhaps something that did not go quite right during the day, or even a great tragedy that you don't seem able to process — and begin to cover it, if you can, with a circuitous layer of peace-seeking thought.

Call it self-healing. Call it acceptance of the real. Call it a widening of perspective, or a submission to whatever-will-be — as in the song "Hi, Lily. Whatever will be, will be."

Oysters, as everyone knows, produce perhaps the most beautiful gems in the world by accident. Without that accidental grain of sand or briny irritation, which they cover within their shells little by little with a circular layer of lustrous nacre, there would be no pearls. And oysters never even get out of bed.

Can we imagine a world without pearls? Ironically, that would be our world were it not for those underwater accidents and the oyster's almost miraculous ability to turn an anomaly into a wonder. Oysters will even create pearls when humans deliberately cause the anomaly, thus producing "cultured" pearls.

Today's little praxis might become more than just a helpful way to go to sleep. At other times of day or night, meditation and mindfulness can begin to surround some of the painful memories of our life not with answers but with acceptance, submission and prayer. Martin Luther King taught that "unmerited suffering is redemptive." Thus, he invites us to grow pearls.

We oppose evil with all our strength when we can. When we can't, life expects us to surrender to its mysteries — and even, by "growing pearls," to try to make something beautiful out of them.

If we can succeed, shall we not arrive at the gates of eternal life looking pretty dandy? Ah, maybe we have figured out why God has made them "pearly gates."

The best way to cheer yourself up is to try to cheer somebody else up.

—**Mark Twain**

A Newt's Novena

No style of prayer is so weird that God can't hear it

It's not that I trust in novenas!
Good God! But what else can I do?
    So often I've prayed
    All in vain, I'm afraid:
Nine prayers in a row might get through.

So my first prayer's to be less "endangered"!
My second — to always find love!
    My third fond request
    Is to not be named "Pest,"
And my fourth is to fly — like a dove!

(Excuse my presumption, Creator,
But to creep like a lizard's a bore.
    My body meanders
    Like all salamanders'
While my spirit is longing to soar!)

My fifth prayer is not to have scales
That are loathsome, repulsive and wrong!
    My sixth fond petition:
    For years I've been wishin'
To grow more than 4-inches long!

My seventh and eighth prayer intentions
Are to change to some two-parted name,
    Like Jack Daw or Ca-nute,
    For this single sound "Newt" —
Suggests "Gingrich" be added for fame.

My ninth prayer: Add more magic powers
Like the miracle feat I can do:
    (Should I lose a limb
    While I'm having a swim
I can grow one that's utterly new!)

Dear God, warm with slime and affection,
Hear nine prayers from a lizard that's cute.
    All I'm asking, it seems:
    Just fulfill all my dreams!
Your affectionate underling,
Newt.

FOOTNOTE — Unstable Delicate Legs

A newt is a small, brash, colorful amphibian with a svelte body, thin skin, and four very frail legs. Its quick darting motion is accomplished largely by slithering. Newt parenting is begun carefully: The tiny eggs are glued one-by-one on leaves of underwater plants. The young begin life breathing like fish, through gills, then later move on to lungs and take to land. They frequently grow fresh new skin and slither right out of their old set, never looking back.

Praxis for Today:

Be a Little Superstitious

Doing something exactly nine times — as in a novena (*novus* means nine) — may help one's concentration, but to think there is something powerful in the nine-fold repetition itself is superstitious. Superstition is defined as "the belief that some action not logically related to a course of events influences its outcome." For instance, to think something you do — like opening an umbrella indoors — influences your life negatively is called superstitious.

Some people really think superstitiously about their prayers: for instance, that mere words of praying can help the sick — and not the inner caring that should go along with it. That is unjustifiably superstitious and makes a prayer into magical words.

Prayer works in mysterious ways, they say, but one of those ways is not automatically. Instead, it may well be that the energy in caring has a lot to do with successfully praying for the sick. If we really care about people, the energy may do its healing with or without the prayer words. If we have a caring heart, we do good wherever we go.

Probably people who caringly spend time together — sleeping together, for instance — have a healthful and healing influence on each other. Animal pets usually care deeply about us: They probably help us more than we know. Pet dogs and cats give us love lessons all the time and educate our hearts in ways that can last a lifetime.

If you want to influence the world for good, practice caring about it, starting today. Take time to care about war and unfairness, needy children or hurting elders, and especially our suffering earth, its drained and decaying wetlands, its gasping atmosphere, its increasingly toxic ground water. Cultivate a healthy superstition about the effect of your feelings. Your feelings matter — and if they lead you to pick up the phone, write a note or join in a political demonstration, so much the better.

The best way to know God is to love many things.

—Vincent van Gogh

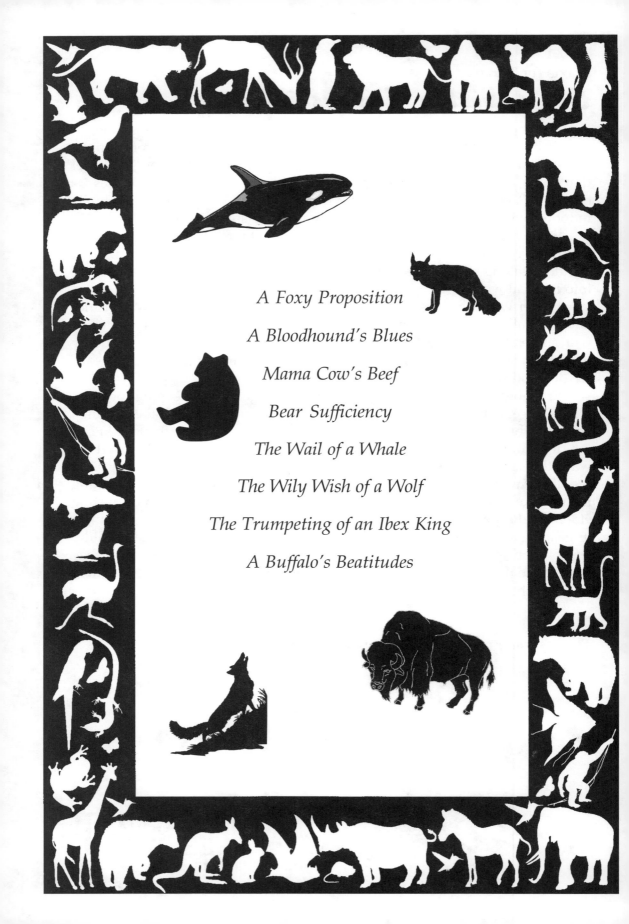

A Foxy Proposition

A Bloodhound's Blues

Mama Cow's Beef

Bear Sufficiency

The Wail of a Whale

The Wily Wish of a Wolf

The Trumpeting of an Ibex King

A Buffalo's Beatitudes

IV.
Almost All Animals Speak . . .

Almost all animals speak. They speak in codes that we do not understand at first. They speak about danger and mates and young. They speak of life and death, of life coming out of life. Much of their passion is embedded in these signals that they send out to the world. With all our intelligence we hear these signals and strain to decipher the codes. We live in a world of messengers that we have only begun to hear.

—Joseph Mortenson in *Whale Songs and Wasp Maps*

A Foxy Proposition

It is foolish to overestimate one's ability to resist temptation

Dear God, though stories show the fox
As sly prevaricator,
In prayers like this, we tell the truth,
For you are our Creator.

You made us what we are today,
I hope you're satisfied.
Before your face, deceit won't work:
There's nothing we can hide.

So in return for honesty
And prayer, sincere and right,
We pray that you'll give us the job
To guard the hens at night!

Don't laugh! Dear God, unless you trust
The foxes you have made,
We'll always lack true self-esteem
And judge ourselves low grade!

So show your glory, Holy One,
And make your honor glow!
We'll guard the hens, you trust our strength
To sniff, then just say NO!

 FOOTNOTE – Smells with Its Tail

The fox is a bushy-tailed, self-possessed member of the dog family, but one capable of climbing small trees. Its cry is hesitant and judicious, just enough to communicate, not enough to get undesirable attention. The fox usually lives in a burrow craftily taken over from a badger or a woodchuck, and it can move swiftly enough to catch a bird or a dodging rabbit. Its vision is superb, and its sense of smell amazing, assisted by an extra scent gland located on its tail. Its hearing is so sharp it is said to be able to detect a delicious mouse whispering 100 yards away.

Praxis for Today:
Be a Saint for a Day

If a fox can daydream of such holiness and self-control as to successfully guard a hen house, perhaps you can experiment with saintliness too.

In a recent very successful and popular book, *Good Enough Catholic*, author Paul Wilkes suggests that in meditating on being saintly one might imagine oneself in a roman collar. It's supposedly a sign of holiness.

People who regularly wear roman collars, however, will tell you in all honesty that "it doesn't really work."

Still, it is an illuminating suggestion, but let's take it a few steps further.

Imagine your saintly self going out on a dream walk wearing your roman collar (even women wear them these days), with two vested acolytes ahead of you carrying candles. A choir follows, chanting in Latin. Police hold back the awed onlookers ahead, as your faithful devotees wave a flag with your name and escutcheon on it that says "Holiness cometh ...." As you move solemnly along, people bow humbly before your saintly presence. Everyone smiles, and all hold out their hands, craving your healing touch. You reach out and place your hand on heads here and there, smiling benevolently, giving the "V" sign in all directions with your fingers, your other hand on your heart.

Besides your roman collar, you wear a long cardinal-red and white robe with side-boys holding its train, and on your head sits a papal tiara, its three points pointing to heaven — where, of course, your thoughts are always located. Your eyes constantly flutter as you gaze heavenward.

But wait! There in the crowd you see the smiling face of Nelson Mandela, the South African hero of forgiveness and reconciliation; next to him and waving at you are Dorothy Day and Mother Teresa, then Rosa Parks and Martin Luther King. How silly you feel in all your saintly splendor. You escape your embarrassment into your waiting stand-up limousine, and you see before you on the wall two buttons marked: **(1)** continue being a "Paul Wilkes type" saint, **(2)** return to normalcy. Which would you press?

It is only a fool who has never felt like one.
> — **Noah ben Shea**

A Bloodhound's Blues

>>><<<->>><<<

A spiritual search usually involves some measure of waiting

>>><<<->>><<<

ARF!
Wait!
I'm worn out tracking thee.
Escaping Spirit, wait for me!
Beyond my reach, beyond my call,
You act like you're not there at all!

WAIT!
God of Living and of Dead!
I've got thy scent stuck in my head.
You smell of Love, the Good, the True:
All I'm created to pursue!

I know the way you must have gone,
You've left your tracks across the dawn.
They smell of meaning, hope and dread.
But where are you? Might you be dead?
    No! You're the font and source of health!
    You're Life! Alive with Life Itself!
Undoubtedly you're everywhere!
Why can't I track you to your lair?

ARF!
Can you hear me in pursuit?
But, Wait! Is chasing so astute?
If I stay calm
and worry-free,
Will you
perhaps
catch up
with
me?

 FOOTNOTE – Astonishing Nose

A bloodhound is an amiable, middle-sized, shorthaired dog, usually black or tan in color with an expressive wizened face, and long, dignified ears. In spite of its name, a bloodhound is in no way vicious or particularly carnivorous. Its distinctive voice is not meant to be threatening, just an expression of excitement in tracking its quarry. Its sense of smell is astonishing, being able to detect, even after many hours, a slight body aroma brushed onto bushes or a foot scent along the ground. Escaping convicts, take a bath!

Praxis for Today:

Let God Catch Up with You

Most of us know that it is wise at times to stop every kind of striving, every kind of yearning, every kind of building — and even communicating — and throw away a period of time on silence and solitude, resting in the present moment in purposeless simplicity. But that's not easy.

Here's one way to "rest." Try it today.

Listen to your body, watch and hear your imagination's screen, be totally in the place where you are. Be here now: That's the secret to a special kind of awakening. This has even been called a kind of prayer, a prayer beyond words or images, simply "waiting for God."

The busy civilized world pressing around us on every side usually pushes us in the opposite direction: Use each moment purposefully! Be all you can be! Your work is never done!

In this exercise, we say *No* to the civilized world, and *Yes* to the Divine Mystery surrounding and inhabiting us with loving kindness, caringness, creating love and infinite compassion — not that we know what any of those divine qualities really means, but they point toward meaning. Feeling their truth is an act of faith, and we can feel their truth most when we stop "doing" and simply wait.

Wait for God, the Unconditionally Loving Parent, the pursuing "Hound of Heaven" (in the words of poet Francis Thompson), our God. Stop for awhile. Let God catch up with you.

The good and the wise lead quiet lives.

— Euripides

BLOODHOUND

Mama Cow's Beef

⋙⋘⋙⋘

Mourning and complaining can become valuable prayers

⋙⋘⋙⋘

My heart is sad, my MOOOOd is black,
The MOOOOn is down, alas, alack.
No hopeful MOOOve do I approve,
The question's MOOOOt, my hope is slack.

My beef? Dear God: my life! my dream!
Where are my calves! Where goes my cream?
  The fleas, the flies,
  These I despise!
But loss of young! A grief supreme!

Men push us out at crack of dawn,
When we come home, our calves are gone!
  We think: How long
  Can this go on?
They think: Calfskin! Veal Parmesan!

I chew my cud and ruminate
The sad disaster of my fate,
  A mother's heart
  All torn apart!
While growing old and overweight.

Some papal bulls bray: Don't Complain!
(Though death and separation reign)
  And saints advise
  "God's ways are wise:
Somehow new life will always rise."

But others say the question's MOOOOOt,
No cow can dig to mystery's root!
  Whatever's true,
  I see why You
Don't answer every time we MOOOOOO!

🐾🐾🐾 FOOTNOTE – A Billion Now on Earth

A cow is the female adult of the bovine family, and roughly a billion of them are standing about on earth, chewing their cud and enjoying the weather. Half are raised strictly for beef, and the other half for milk and its products. "Veal" is the name given to the meat of calves that are slaughtered at less than three months old. Most cows have a coat of short hair that grows thicker and longer in the winter. A cow is usually taciturn and calls out only when it definitely has something to moo about.

Praxis for Today:

Learn to "Un-Pray"

Among the 150 psalms in our Bible are many that express complaints, and these biblical prayers may be a model for us. For instance, Psalm 119 complains: "O God, do not take the word of truth out of my mouth!" In Psalm 139: "If thou wouldst but slay the wicked, O God, the men of blood would depart from me!" And Psalm 144: "Hide not thy face from me lest I die...." The book of Habakkuk begins, "How long, O Lord, must I cry for help and you not hear?"

Complaining seems almost the opposite of praying: It is "unpraying." But it works — in the sense that it enables us to speak honestly to God, especially when we feel unnecessarily hurt, unlucky, lost or angry.

Doctor of the Church, St. Thomas Aquinas, stated in the thirteenth century that it is legitimate to pray for anything that it is legitimate to want. That means, firstly, that it is not okay to pray to own your neighbor's hot tub, but it is okay to ask to be as successful as she is. This may at first seem to be a pretty abstruse distinction, but they imply, in fact, two very different kinds of prayer.

The point is that we need not be intensely cautious in talking to God, frightened that if we say the wrong thing, we may be hit by lightning.

Our true God is mostly mystery, and no one can say for certain how a prayer may affect God's heart. Modern spiritual writers speak as if God is unable to do certain things: save the Jews from the Shoah, prevent foolish human decisions from having their natural consequences, force the Haves to share with the Have-nots. These prayers do not have their intended effect, writers say, because God did not create that kind of a world for us.

Still, faithful people feel free to complain to God about things like this — for complaining is still an opening of the heart, and that is the very purpose of prayer.

Mystic and genius Anthony de Mello asks: Is your love of God secure enough that you can rage against him? The question is a good test of our spirituality.

So bring your complaints to God in prayer. Like Mama Cow, we may sometimes come to see that there are some advantages for us in the way things are — and the rest is mystery.

> *Trouble is the first path to truth.*
>
> **—Lord Byron**

Bear Sufficiency

–»»‹‹‹–»»‹‹‹–

Rejoice to have enough of the essentials of life

–»»‹‹‹–»»‹‹‹–

Thanks, but no thanks, O God, my God,
Enough's enough for me.
I've fur, fat, cubs and fish to eat:
That's a sufficiency.

You need not add a honeycomb,
That most amazing grace.
Enough's your breeze that cools my hide,
Your sun that warms my face.

Some bears, you know, grow 9-feet tall,
Weigh fifteen hundred pounds,
While others are petite and quick;
But all of us are round . . .

. . . Especially round when winter comes:
We hunker down and snore
Through months of blizzards, ice and storm.
(Bleak weather is a bore!)

Come, God, and snuggle down with me
Here in my deepest den.
We'll snooze together till the world
Is bear-able again.

FOOTNOTE – Walking with Bear Feet

A bear is a rambunctious animal with thick, shaggy fur and coming in a variety of sizes: some species just 60 pounds, some up to 1,500. They usually prefer to live alone, not in familial packs, and exist only north of the equator. A bear's assorted heavy growls are nuanced in intent, but usually are just chilling to humans. Bear feet have five toes, each toe topped with a long, vicious claw. They are meat-eating creatures, and while trainable for human entertainment, can never be absolutely trusted. Unlike most animals, bears walk flat-footed, giving them a distinctive but not slow gait. Grizzlies, for instance, can outsprint a racehorse if they have to.

Think of Yourself as a Fetus

It is really not so extraordinary that bears enjoy hibernating in a dark den. Life in the dark is something each of us experienced in our mother's womb. We emerge into the light, but the mysteries do not go away — they intensify.

Some philosophers have described our mystery-filled, often difficult and unsatisfying life on earth as similar to that of a mature fetus waiting to be born, bewildered by its plight.

Imagine that for a moment. In the darkness of the womb, we experience some motions and sounds that make us anxious. We are not really alone. We are intrigued by the other presences just a thin wall of skin away — ever close to us — and by the sounds and music we hear.

At times we feel comfortable and content, yet we have little hands that can explore, for instance, our muscular legs. (What are they for?) And then, our eye sockets, our ears. (Total mystery!) We move about pleasurably and obviously are being carried from place to place, but what is that all about? Where are we going?

What might occur to us in womb-consciousness: Might the explanation of these mysteries be that we are really designed for some kind of "other world," a world of something other than darkness and "womb temperature"?

We know very little of pain, and a great deal about sleep, but what kind of dreams do we have? Can we let ourselves go to sleep and put our trust in our world? Were we insightful enough to imagine a God, would God not be like the mother in whom we live and move and have our being?

Somewhere in our subconscious do we not have such paradigms? Dig into your deepest memories, and for awhile today imagine yourself again a contented fetus. Enjoy the surrounding world of love, having a sufficiency of every important need — but bathed in mysteries and contradictions not unlike the world we know.

Love sought is good, but given unsought is better.

—**William Shakespeare**

The Wail of a Whale

It is futile to try to become something other than we are

Life is not easy, Holy One,
    For whales here in the ocean,
One hundred twenty feet in length,
    A blubber-blob in motion.

    Old dinosaurs grew 90 feet
    But then their growth would quit.
    Blue whales are bigger! In our mouths
    An elephant would fit!

Yet we've no teeth! We dine on krill:
    More creatures ought to try it!
Too wee to see, krill makes you fat
    No matter how you diet.

    (Since I grow large on teeny fish,
    Mere microscopic elements,
    Would I grow smaller if I ate
    Large buffalo and elephants?)

Some 40 million years ago
    My ancestors went swimming,
And ended up becoming whales
    Who have this problem slimming.

    Please make me smaller, Holy One,
    And I will sing your glory
    And smack my tail as applause
    For my weight-losing story.

My heart will beat with love for thee,
Though it beats rather slowly,
Nine times a minute is my pulse,
A pace serene and holy.

    So hear my prayer and help me shrink,
    And feel less irritation,
    And leap more high above the waves
    To show my exaltation.

FOOTNOTE — A Toothless Giant

A whale is an affectionate, warm-blooded, fish-like mammal that breathes air, bears live young and lives in oceans all over the world. Whales sing in many modes, clicks and songs that can be detected by other whales as far away as four miles. Though they are toothless and dine only on fish almost invisibly tiny (called krill), they still grow bulky. The blue whale is the largest animal that has ever lived on earth, up to 120 feet long (but won't tell you its weight).

Praxis for Today:

Enjoy Life as It Is

Though human life is necessarily difficult, it need not be other than fundamentally and habitually joyous. Even Job returned to a life of joy when his famous travails were over.

We are sublimely loved by God, and if we have care for other people, other people will, in turn, have care for us. It is always a joy to see in someone's eyes a genuine affection for us. We need it as much as we need air or water.

Laced into everything is a strain of the joyous. "The world is charged with the grandeur of God," wrote Gerard Manley Hopkins, the mystic and poet. He added that God's grandeur flashes and oozes and sparks out everywhere — if we are alert to it.

It is mindfulness that produces such alertness — taking time to stop awhile and simply be present.

Then, whenever we perceive that grandeur flashing out in the avalanche of brilliance and music from someone's singing voice, for instance, we might learn to shout, "Yes!" (to God) in our hearts.

In early morning, it's another day: Yes! Taste that apple: Yes! Hear that dove: Yes! There's the phone: Yes! I have work to do: Yes! Life: Yes!

Resting feels good? My co-worker is courageous? My digestion is working? Yes! Yes! Yes! Time to slow down: Okay! Time to cook: Okay! There's the call to care: Yes! There's the call to be care-ful: Yes!

If out of mindfulness we learn to have ears to hear, then there's the song coming from the earth too: Take my air to breathe! Here is nourishing food to eat! Have water, have milk, have wine! And someday perhaps we'll hear that song recapitulated in a minor key: Now, give your body back to me where it came from and grew from: Yes! Yes! Okay! Okay! Here comes the future: Let it happen! In mindfulness, we affirm it all.

Suffering becomes beautiful when a person bears great sorrows with cheerfulness, not through insensitivity but through largeness of mind.

— **Aristotle**

WHALE

The Wily Wish of a Wolf

Bad reputations are often well deserved

I much regret, O Lord Divine,
The reputation that is mine:
Lies and untruths become a flood
Until one's name is worse than mud.

Wolves, folks are told, are vicious beasts
Who turn chance meetings into feasts,
Crafty and cunning from our birth,
Who in sheep's clothing roam the earth
Seeking something to devour —
Whatever falls within our power.

Nothing's farther from the truth!
Great God, we're gentle from our youth,
Wolf packs are villages of love
Where young and old fit hand-in-glove.

Unlike wild beasts, we mate for life
And raise our puppies without strife.
For food, wolves follow earth's menu,
The same as doves and lovebirds do.

We're crafty? Please, dear God, get real!
Come to our den and have a meal!
Cocktails are at half past three.
What's for dinner?
Wait and see!

 FOOTNOTE — Just the World's Largest Dog

The wolf is the largest member of the dog family and varies in color all the way from white to black. It is famous for its nocturnal howl: eerie, ominous, ghostly. Wolves live in families of five to fifteen, which are based around a dominant pair and ruled by a strict domestic hierarchy in which rascals are excommunicated. Wolves hunt in packs, and their favorite meals out are elk, deer, bison and mountain sheep.

Praxis for Today:

Pray for Your Worst Enemies

It is healthy to admit that there are some people we do not like, people we dread being near, people who give us a mysterious inner pain. With a little stretch of the language, you may call them your "enemies." We may even live near genuinely dangerous people — whose reputations threaten us. They should all be recipients of our prayers and genuine good wishes.

To clarify our thoughts it helps to name and recognize those whom we may claim we love in some way, but whom we certainly don't like.

"Love your enemies," said Jesus. "Do good to those who hate you."

Perhaps there is one particular person who comes to mind, perhaps a few. Here is a prayer that — if you say it and mean it — will help you achieve forgiveness of your enemies:

> Holy Creator, bless all my enemies with joy and wisdom.
> May they never suffer punishment for whatever they have done wrong
>   except insofar as it may enlighten and enrich their heart.
> Forgive them, Holy One, and empower me also to forgive them.
> Surround them with success and human fulfillment.
> And as I forgive them in my heart of hearts,
>   so may I be forgiven before you
>   for whatever small-souledness, injustice or human sin
>   I may have committed.
>   Amen.

And remember: This is the only way absolution comes about, according to Jesus.

Hatred does not cease by hatred, but only by love; this is an eternal rule.
—Buddha

WOLF

The Trumpeting of an Ibex King

We inevitably imagine God to be very much like ourselves

God Triumphant!
Lord!
Sky King!
Commander-in-Chief of Everything!
Almighty Potentate on High,
With horns that reach up to the sky!
    Thy beard is fearsome, long and round,
    You leap whole Alps in a single bound,
    You snort typhoons when you feel glum
    And butt all foes to kingdom come.

I'm King of the Mountaintop, like you,
Made in your image and likeness, too,
But I bow my 30-inch horns down low,
My full submission to you to show.
    (I know how discipline can decay
    When lesser creatures disobey.
    I too have rules no one may flout,
    And dogmas there are no doubts about.)

I'm glad you have no Goddess Peer
Some *Female* Equal to revere!
One small in size with almond eyes
And thoughts that challenge the strong and wise!
    With Son and Ghost, you Males are three,
    But united as one essentially:
    One Lone Male Monarch with horns uncurled:
    A PERFECT GOD FOR A HE-GOAT'S WORLD!

 FOOTNOTE — Only the Males Have Beards

The ibex is a large, arrogant wild goat found mostly high in the mountains of Asia. Its coat is shorthaired and kempt. Males have a gallant white beard (unlike females) and decisive horns towering as much as 36 inches above their heads, twice the size of the females. Peculiarly, the males live and graze together, apart from the refining influence of the females and the young. The trumpeting call of full-grown males can make the Asian mountain valleys echo for miles.

Praxis for Today:

Imagine Yourself the Other Sex

Stand before a mirror today and imagine yourself the opposite sex.

First, put stereotypes aside: It is too easy to *masquerade* as the other sex, to pretend, to trivialize. Instead, really switch everything, your bodily differences and hair styles, then your soul differences, then your role in the world, your new vulnerabilities, the societal expectations with which you are burdened.

This is a meditation: Take your time. Look into your own true eyes but give yourself everything else new, even a new name. Say hello to your new self now in a different voice — newly isolated in the world, if you've become male; newly disempowered, if you've become female. How does it feel?

However the exercise goes for you, you surely will have to deal with something of the mystery hidden within our differing sexualities, one of the great unknowns in everyone's life. What attitude would you now take toward the newly "opposite sex," toward homosexuality, toward reproductive questions?

How would you feel now before the eyes of God? Do you now more resemble "the Lord God"? How would you tend to create the perfect God for yourself?

If you can't get yourself to even think of trying this exercise, does it not say something important about your attitude toward the other gender?

The most beautiful experience we can have is the mysterious. It is the fundamental emotion which stands at the cradle of true art and true science.

— Albert Einstein

A Buffalo's Beatitudes

To simply be useful is a noble life ambition

Blessed are those of humble horn
    for theirs is a prairie of blessing.
Blessed are those of low-slung head
    for they shall find greens and water.
Blessed are the meek and peaceful of hoof
    for they shall be beloved.
Blessed are the thick-skinned and shaggy
    for they shall be blankets of warmth.

Blessed are the stew-makers
    for they shall be much sought after.
Blessed are the edible
    for they shall see God.
Blessed are those who are pursued for hunger's sake
    for they shall be called gifts of the Most High.
Blessed are those of humble horn
    for theirs is a prairie of blessing.

 FOOTNOTE — A Hum of Contentment

Buffalo are cattle-like, peace-loving wild oxen who live on plains in many parts of the earth. Those in the American West are more properly called "bison." They are sociable and communicative animals, and a herd will utter a great communal hum when all is well. In 1850 an estimated 20 million buffalo roamed the western plains, but they were so easy to hunt and so useful to humankind, that by 1899 uncontrolled hunting had left less than 600 alive. Today their numbers are increasing every year, and limited and respectful hunting is encouraged again.

Praxis for Today:

Honor the Ordinary

As the placid buffalo seem to have no individualistic ambition, they model a virtuous life we might call "ordinary." Ethician Daniel Maguire claims that holiness — which is just another word for extraordinary human goodness — is not normally based on some intense sense of the divine, or desire for a heavenly reward or some kind of perfect submission to human customs and ethical expectations.

It all starts, he says, in "the mystery-laden discovery of the value of persons."

Thus, the best people among us humans are those who have learned how astonishingly precious are those they love.

This, says Maguire, is always "an affective faith experience" that can come and go, grow and recede.

How mothers feel about their children, for instance, is a perfect basis for holiness. So precious are these children (and therefore all children, including the grown-up ones) that heroic work for their welfare becomes possible, and lifelong belief in their value bursts out naturally.

The same can be said of people who have fallen in love. It is a faith experience — faith in someone's preciousness. Saints/Lovers: We seldom put those ideas together. But, if Maguire is right, they belong together.

So in your pursuit of human fulfillment, you need the experience of admiring someone, of being awed by someone's beauty, of caring very strongly for someone, strongly enough perhaps to die, or to live, for them — in order to know, to taste, how valuable people can be.

We need such experience in order to lay the foundation of a moral life that is first-hand (or real) and not second-hand (and artificial). We may spend life behaving well, but if we don't do so passionately, and thus lovingly, it is a second-hand life.

So only the experience of love can enable us to choose to be deeply good and deeply dedicated to goodness. And if love hasn't found you lately, you can and should go in search of it. It can lead to holiness like nothing else can.

It is only with the heart that one can see rightly. What is essential is invisible to the eye.

—Saint-Exupery

The Dirge of a Dinosaur

An Eel's Appeal

Psalm of a Sorry Starfish

Twelve Steps of a Saltaholic

Confessions of a Jellyfish

A Hearing for a Herring

Allegations of an Alligator

A Lemming's Lament

V. Both Ancestors and Companions...

The animals on this earth are both our ancestors and our companions.

—Lawrence Binder in *Earth Prayers*

The Dirge of a Dinosaur

-»»«-»»«-

Nothing so intrigues the mind as the seemingly absurd

-»»«-»»«-

Holy One, Creating Mystery,
See, at last I turn to thee,
In despair to see my fellow
Dinosaurs in agony.

Death has conquered all our nations,
Overthrown at his command,
Killing dinosaurs by millions,
Misery fills every land.

How can you allow this carnage?
Did you not call us to life?
. . . Watch the fascinating drama
Of our living and our strife?

. . . Guide our evolution till we
Prospered many million years?
Why would you allow this failure?
Even memory disappears!

Silent God, come live within us
Even now beneath this sky
Where the final darkness gathers
Every hour — we know not why.

Make our deaths a revelation
To all things that live and die:
You are sovereign in creation —
It's no use to question why.

FOOTNOTE — Every Last One Has Now Disappeared

The dinosaurs dominated this earth for 140 million years, ranging from species of chicken size to 90-foot long beasts, three stories high and weighing 160,000 fierce pounds, shaking the earth with every thunderous step. They lived successfully all over the planet, nourishing themselves on the tasty edibles that earth provided (including each other). Then, suddenly, within a few years, they were completely gone, all of them dead. Only their bones, and multisyllabic names, exist today.

Praxis for Today:
Listen for the Voices of God

The voices of God are multiple, speaking in our own sorrows and successes, in all of life. To hear the voices of God, don't only listen for someone calling in the night — as Samuel did. Attend instead to all the forces of evolution: the surging vibrations of change and discovery, of hopeful creativity and inventive optimism. God is speaking there.

It's true: The mystery that enfolds us speaks in the voice of real events — human and cosmic — in the songs of prophetesses and prophets, in the identification of evil wherever it is found — and in the courage to leave despair behind and invent a never-tried-before future.

While we truly stand on the shoulders of giants, we have to pick and choose among the shoulders available. Traditions, like recipes, can be helpful. We build on some of them. Other recipes we reject for they have proved inadequate, and sometimes even poisonous. We need no more religions, for instance, that insist that God can only be imagined as male.

One great modern prophet is the self-styled "geologian" Thomas Berry. Here is a summary of his fondest dream that we will hear the voice of God shaping a new dream right in our genetic coding:

> A new revelatory experience is needed, an experience wherein human consciousness awakens to the grandeur and sacred quality of the Earth process. This awakening is our human participation in the dream of the Earth, the dream that is carried in … the depths of our genetic coding. Therein the Earth functions at a depth beyond our capacity for conscious awareness…. Such participation in the dream of the Earth we probably have not had since our earlier shamanic times, but therein lies our hope for the future for ourselves and for the entire Earth community.

To take part in the dream of the earth, we have to dream; for dreams — and only dreams — connect our hearts to God. Even the "Our Father," for all its parochialism, may be seen as seven world-changing dreams. Dreams (or call it desire) link us to evolution itself, or Evolution Herself. The protozoa dreamed of adventure, the dinosaurs dreamed of flying, the great apes dreamed true love awake. Everything is possible if we can only dream abundantly.

It is difficult to say what is impossible, for the dream of yesterday is the hope of today and the reality of tomorrow.
> **—Robert H. Goddard**

DINOSAUR

An Eel's Appeal

>>><<<>>><<<

When envying others, remember the gifts you have

>>><<<>>><<<

Hearing prayers today?
I have a few to say:
    It's me, a snaky eel here in the mud.
Don't look away, dear Lord,
As if you're feeling bored.
    I'm an embarrassment? A flop? A dud?

I'm s'posed to be a fish!
Not weird and outlandish,
    A snake-like wriggling monster 6-feet long!
All slime from toe to head
With jolts that shock you dead
    Should you quite accidentally touch me wrong.

My prayer and my appeal
Is, please, just make me real,
    The kind of fish I can be proud to be:
A pike or cod or flounder,
Perhaps a dozen pounder
    Who roams the deepest mysteries of the sea.

What nonsense is an eel!
A creepy crawly deal!
    Like nothing else that slithers on the earth!
O Nature's Artisan,
Please redesign my plan,
    And I will praise your name for all I'm worth.

But if I'm out of line
And irk you when I whine,
    I take it back, and humbly change my creed.
We eels have one thing nice:
No prig gives us advice
    Or tries to change the shocking life we lead.

FOOTNOTE — Ten-Feet Long with Canine Teeth

The eel is an elongated fish with a snake-like body, smooth, slimy skin and usually no scales. Most live in fresh water. Many grow to about 3 feet in length, but an adult conger eel can be 10-feet long and weigh 140 pounds. An electric eel can generate 600 volts and stun even very large animals. The moray eel, mysteriously, is striped like a zebra and has a large head with rounded nostrils, strong jaws and canine-like teeth. Some mother eels can produce roughly eight million eggs at a time, but seldom is anyone counting.

Praxis for Today:
Practice Shocking People

Life needs spice, variety and the unexpected.

Have you ever encountered one of those wonderful people who habitually surprise their friends with unexpected "appreciations" or greeting cards out of the blue?

Try it yourself today as a spiritual exercise: Put some spirit into the life of those around you. Could you not shock even someone quite close to you with a surprise gift or greeting?

Love companions, alas, can begin to take each other for granted. It's as if to say: Your love for me was given and granted once upon a time ... so I need not take care to win it over and over. Often that is exactly the opposite of the truth.

The truth is that love, like a garden, grows better the more you take care of it. So once in awhile surprise a longtime friend or spouse with some shocking show of affection.

Or, shock your relatives by being unexpectedly honest and open. Spice up their lives sometime with the naked and unadorned truth. Just as nudists do all the time, once in awhile don't clothe your words in loose, ill-fitting metaphors and euphemisms, but say the plain truth right out.

Tell your honest feelings: "I'm feeling so confused .... I feel furious .... I'm way too sentimental about .... I hate to admit that ...." Often the conversation will be a lot more important for everyone, all shocked into a truer and, therefore, more interesting reality.

Make yourself an honest person, and then you can be sure there is one less rascal in the world.

—Thomas Carlyle

Psalm of a Sorry Starfish

Things are seldom what they seem

Twinkle, twinkle (starfish pray),
How we wonder what to say.
   Deep below the waves we be,
   Like lost diamonds in the sea:
Twinkle, twinkle, hear us pray,
Cheerless, wrapt in dark dismay.

We don't twinkle! We're no star!
Look at us! We're just bizarre!
   Not a star and not a fish,
   To be either, don't we wish!
God of all that's picturesque,
Why've you made us so grotesque?

We must creep in oyster beds,
Scaring all those sleepyheads,
   Opening their shell-door seal
   Just enough to have a meal.
They must die so we survive!
What a way to stay alive!

Five to fifty arms have we,
Made to grab an enemy,
   Tiny eyespots on each tip,
   Let's us look before we nip!
Mother Ocean, God Above,
Could we not lead lives of love?

   Bright and friendly we would be,
   Saintly stars beneath the sea,
      Or in heaven let us dwell
      In the sky from whence we fell.
   God of all who swim or creep,
   Hear us — as deep calls unto deep.

 FOOTNOTE — Little Suction-Cup Feet

The starfish is an exotic sea animal (not a fish) that usually lounges lazily on the sea floor and stretches out its many arm-like extensions in the shape of a shining star or the sun and its rays. The starfish "sees" with a small colored eyespot located at the tip of each arm and is equipped with suction-cup feet that extend from its mouth to each arm tip. Starfish are vigorous, energetic and resourceful, and even if cut in two, each piece will regenerate into a whole new animal if you give it half a chance.

Praxis for Today:
See Your Beautiful Side

Many people wish they were other than what they are: stars, winners, celebrities. But perhaps your celebrity day is coming: your funeral.

Funerals can be astonishing. Modern funerals often include opportunities for friends and family to speak, and we often get to hear amazing and comforting things about the deceased: how generously they treated people in need, what wonderful words they said one day, how important they were to this person and that person.

It is helpful to imagine ourselves at our own funeral once in awhile.

Admittedly, at our funeral people will likely only speak of our strengths, our best moments, our most thoughtful words. But that is surely the way our God sees us not through the eyes of a human judge but through the eyes of a loving parent, or — closer to the truth — a loving, indulgent grandparent.

Meditate on the kind of words people might say at your funeral, supposing you were to die today. Put such a eulogy into actual words. "He was a compassionate person ...." "She had a listening heart ...." "He strove mightily to be a good parent ...." "She could be wonderful fun."

Alice Walker has said that the only God deserving of worship would be one who worships us. So dream up the words of worship that might be said of YOU .... Then think about yourself today as just a little bit "worshipful."

The gods conceal from humans the happiness of death, that they may endure life.

—Lucan

The Twelve Steps of a Saltaholic

—»»«««—»»«««—

The heroic journey out of addiction requires courage — and other people

—»»«««—»»«««—

My name is Sam and I'm a saltaholic!
Thou art the "Higher Power" I acclaim!
I turn from eight years' boozing in this ocean
Back to freshwater streams from which I came.

My salty life has been insane to manage,
So I will take the Twelve Steps to improve:
Down with the life of salt and self-indulgence!
Up with the peace no force on earth can move!

Now is the time to spawn high in a river,
Leaving behind each broken pledge and wish,
Making a list of everyone I've injured
During my years of drinking like a fish.

Now is the time to make my reparations,
Finding a Mentor who can guide my way,
Trusting in friends who also fight addictions:
Salt-free for one more hour! Then one more day!

No more life in the fast lane of the Gulf Stream
Where I would race at twenty-five an hour.
Finally it's time to get my life together,
Looking for courage from thee, Higher Power!

Maybe before I make this holy journey
I can give help to some lost, hopeless fish
Who will put saltaholism behind him
With my encouragement and prayerful wish.

Though I've grown 5-feet long, an 80 pounder,
These final days will be my very best,
Climbing high waterfalls, past bears and rapids —
There to give life — then lay my own to rest.

🐾🐾🖐 FOOTNOTE – The Lower Jaw Grows a Vicious Hook

The salmon is a large, valorous Atlantic-area fish, often silver in color with an impressive pointed head. They are born in freshwater streams, and after two to three years they swim to the ocean where they reside for six to eight years, then return to the freshwater to reproduce. In sockeye salmon, the lower jaw grows into a vicious hook, called a kype, useful in its search for dinner. Breeding males may turn bright red with a green head, advertising the claim to a promising potency.

Praxis for Today:

Lower Your Fences

Psychologists claim we all have some level of addiction, to some kind of need: for security, for unreal hopes, even at times for failure. The worst part of addiction is the way it isolates us. It creates a fence between others and us. Lowering our fences is part of breaking into freedom from addictions.

Fences are symbols packed with meaning. A "spite fence" is built to offend, to keep us away. Communicative neighbors will always find a way to ignore it, to attempt to stay in touch anyway.

An ordinary property-line fence, on the other hand, can be comforting: It helps us not to trespass on a neighbor's land. This is what Robert Frost had in mind in his famous poem "Mending Wall." His neighbor would always say to him, "Good fences make good neighbors," and once a year they would walk the stone fence line together, repairing any breaks. But Frost himself felt "something there is that doesn't love a wall, that wants it down."

His implication is that nature often hates divisions between people, between races, between language groups, between classes of people, like the rich and poor, the educated and uneducated, the young and the old.

Today's praxis is a challenge: to lower fences, taking our cue from Frost, harmonizing with nature in breaking down barriers that stand between other people and ourselves.

Think of someone who possibly feels fenced away from you, perhaps across a fence that was built out of spite or by foolish wishful thinking, or one that came about just by accident. Walk that fence line today and make human contact across the divide. Even though the fence may remain, it will be a little less obstructive, gradually allowing more and more human interaction between you.

You may be surprised at how your neighbor will welcome the new view he gets of who you are.

Let us so live that when we come to die even the undertaker will be sorry.
— **Mark Twain**

SALMON

Confessions of a Jellyfish

⇶⇷⇶⇷

Self-criticism is often erroneous

⇶⇷⇶⇷

O Holy Ocean, Womb of Life,
God of the Bounding Main,
Hear this confession of my faults
And take away my stain.

You'll never put me on your list
Of saints and heroines,
Of creatures tough and firm and sure —
Not me, I'm full of sins.

A Jellyfish! All gush and squish,
No sense of wrong or right,
First, one inch wide, then, with the tide
I grow huge overnight.

I have no backbone and no guts,
No vigor of the will.
I vacillate with every wave,
Un-firm and volatile.

What's that? YOU LOVE ME AS I AM?
"A great transparent wonder?"
"Your tentacles all spark with strength?"
No, God! I'm just a blunder!
A gutless freak! A floating joke!
Not fish! Not made of jelly!
YOU LOVE ME STILL? Don't hate my shape?
Don't find me gross and smelly?

PRAISE GOD, ye ocean freaks and flukes,
Ye frightening creations!
The Love who made us loves us still,
Despite our reputations!

FOOTNOTE — Arms Contain Stinging Cells

Jellyfish are obliging marine animals of many sizes that have a nearly transparent saucer-shaped body. They range from pea size to some 7-feet across, often changing shape dramatically according to how much they eat. Under the umbrella-shaped body hangs a short tube which contains the mouth, and around the mouth are four busy little arms that capture food — and contain stinging cells to stun and subdue small sea animals that are reluctant to come quietly.

Praxis for Today:

Give Thanks for Shortcomings

Is it not our human weaknesses that build the quickest bridge to others?

Contest winners are surrounded by appreciative fans, but those competitive encounters are the opposite of heart-to-heart communions. It is in our role as commoners and mere humans that we make the quickest and best friends, feel our hearts open and even touched.

In superficial introductions we often politely ask, "How are you?" but we definitely don't mean what we ask. We don't expect our new acquaintance to tell us how they really are. We would be shocked if someone replied, "I'm scared — by you," or "I am awful" or, worst of all, "I'd rather not say." Better to say the conventional: "Fine, thanks" — though we don't exactly mean to thank them for anything other than their courtesy.

So if you want to make effective human contact, do not broadcast your strengths, your achievements or your victories. Take off your medals of achievement. Show your wounds instead: your fears, your feelings of inadequacy, your defeats. Everyone loves a loser.

The householders who have everything may never meet their neighbors, but if they lack an egg, they may make new, even lifelong, friends.

I thank God for my handicaps, for through them, I have found myself, my work and my God.

— Helen Keller

JELLYFISH

A Hearing for a Herring

It's painful not to be known by your real name

O Mighty Sea in whom we live and swim,
I ask a hearing in your holy sight.
The plight of baby herring is my import:
How we get named "sardines!" It isn't right!

It's a disgrace in every supermarket,
There tins of "sardines" pile up by the ton,
Yet in the tins are twenty-one-odd species
Of different kinds of creatures named as one.

And that one name does not name any fishes!
There's no "sardine" in your transcendent plan,
And herring all resent the implication
That we were born to squeeze into a can.

Where taste is in the oil, not in the contents,
And oil is far more costly than the fish!
Oh, mighty God, remove this great dishonor;
Do hear our prayer, and grant us what we wish!

For we are born, like every other creature,
To glorify your great and holy name,
And as your name is precious to your honor,
Don't be surprised your children feel the same.

FOOTNOTE – Easy to Catch

The herring is an abundant food fish that grows to about 1-foot long and travels in gigantic schools along the coastal waters of North America and Europe. They have scales usually blue-green on top, brilliant silver on the sides and white below. Herring are easy to catch, a happy circumstance for humans and other fish eaters. Recently it was announced that the Norwegians are catching more herring than are any other fishermen (or women), but the statistic is still unconfirmed by the ocean-roving news shark — who is notoriously hard of herring.

Praxis for Today:
Name Yourself Anew

Though William Shakespeare remarked: "What's in a name?...A rose by any other name would smell as sweet," still names matter mightily.

Ben Franklin wrote essays under the name "Silence DoGood" to make it all more interesting. The impressively named "Helen Hayes" was really someone else, and so were Mark Twain, Bob Hope, Groucho Marx and perhaps even Shakespeare.

So make a spiritual exercise of renaming yourself.

What name would you like across your T-shirt as you come into God's sparkling presence at death? Or even today? What name would fit you, truthfully? "Happy Neverquit"? "Doctor Fail-Prone"? "Mother Listener"? "Grampa Tries-a-Lot"?

Use many words if you like: "Wants-to-understand," "Lonesome-Seeker-Bewildered-but-Uncomplaining." Or, rename yourself based on an animal or plant that fits you: "Whale Whalen," "Bookworm Brown," "Booby Becker" or "Squash Hennessy."

Still, in some ways only God knows our name, that unique-to-us combination of infinitely detailed DNA and human experience that forms our true self. Perhaps if God were to call us by our true name, we might recognize it as our very own. *"What I do* is me," said the poet Gerard Manley Hopkins.

Has God a name for you that includes both what you are and what you have done? Have you spent your life, as Hopkins goes on to suggest, "selving" — that is, becoming yourself, not someone invented by others?

Imagine yourself waiting to be called from St. Peter's waiting room into your after-death self. What combination of words would you recognize as naming your inmost and unique self? "The one who knew I was crazy about her!" "My dear brave one who carried for forty-five years the heavy mystery of a disabled child!" "The one who tamed tigers in her heart!" "My dear deeply bruised mystic!" "Troublemaker!" "Lucky!" "Beautiful!"

Rename yourself for a day. Imagine your true name in God's mind and heart. Then prepare yourself for the thrill of recognition at last. Listen for your name, then walk up and get your Oscar!

The blazing evidence of immortality is our dissatisfaction with any other solution.

—Ralph Waldo Emerson

Both Animals and Companions ♦ 101

Allegations of an Alligator

It is easy to fear the wrong thing

With your permission, God of Deepest Mystery,
Let alligators list their worst complaints:
Why do you scare the world with dreadful creatures?
Don't you feel bad when some scared gator faints?
    Our jaws curve up as if we're always placid:
    Not true! We're patient souls but hardly saints.

For instance, must there be such horrid creatures
As HUMMINGBIRDS within this peaceful place?
They flap their wings at sixty times a second,
A frightful, wild, unworldly, ghastly pace.
    O God, that gives a normal creature nightmares
    And makes a gator's heart a basket case.

Next, GOLDFISH! How they scare us half to death
The way they flash and glisten in the sun,
Their beauty shocking, grizzly, horrifying,
Too awesome to exist, they daze and stun
    Poor alligators, unprepared to witness
    That spooky, dazzling, strange phenomenon.

But worst of all, on banks of darkening rivers
We're frightened by the sight of DUCKLINGS there,
Who quack and peep and chirp their horrid whispers
And fill our hearts with dread and deep despair.
    Great God, why is your world so wild and ruthless,
    While we so long for quiet time for prayer . . .

. . . Some quiet time to have a peaceful supper,
A zebra or a lion or a boar,
Then warm our crusty backside in the sunshine
While we digest that healthful snack, and snore
    And dream of those sweet dinosaur companions
    We played with peacefully in days of yore.

 FOOTNOTE — Easily Frightened

The alligator is a giant reptile resembling an overgrown lizard, but with a thicker body and a large grinning mouth containing many razor-sharp teeth. Alligators once grew 18-feet long but are shorter now, and seldom weigh more than a mere 500 pounds. The American alligator is easily frightened, and is much less vicious than its meaner cousins, the crocodile or the cayman. While once "endangered," they are now reclassified as simply "threatened," though some still feel endangered — like the lily-livered alligator-chicken above.

Praxis for Today:

See Yourself as Fearsome

If you find it hard to think of yourself as threatening to someone, imagine first the kind of qualities you notice in people who are never threatening to you.

Are they not people, first of all, who love you, who smile when they look at you?

Are they not people who know you love them?

Are they not people who would never shame you or cause you any pain?

Are they not people to whom you can speak without constraint, who would never use their power over you to manipulate you into doing something you don't really want to do?

Are they not people whom you do not have to try to please — because your mere existence pleases them?

Pause for a moment and pick out which of your friends are the very least fearsome? Are they not the great saints in your life?

Once you have decided who they are, then it might be useful to just reverse the meditation: Whom do you really fear? Which individuals make you tense up? Who is it who has high expectations of you, who will give you friendly strokes provided you perform in a way satisfactory to them? Who is really a painful acquaintance, someone you would avoid if you could, someone who does not really care two hoots about you?

Consider this: Those people you fear the most may well be those who fear and distrust you the most.

Fear often is a double enemy: It is a painful experience for yourself and for the person that you feel threatened by. On the other hand, "Love overcomes fear," says St. John.

The only sure way not to be fearsome to others is to find a way to start honestly caring about them. Stop worrying about your own status or appearance. Stop shaming behaviors (like bragging or wearing your medals at other peoples' expense), and take more interest in others. Stop being fearsome. Stop seeing others as threatening, but rather see them as afraid, and many of your own fears may fade away.

As a warm-up, explain this approach to the nearest alligator, and then apply the same ideas to your own soul.

Nothing in life is to be feared. It is only to be understood.
                                                    —Marie Curie

Both Animals and Companions ♦ 103

A Lemming's Lament

Urges of the heart need to be governed by reason

Dear God of Love, are you too near?
Causing too much affection
To fill our hearts and body parts
Beyond our circumspection?

We lemmings look like Arctic mice
But win wide admiration
For lions' hearts — and loving arts —
That end... in procreation.

Alas, we overpopulate,
Then migrate in a dither
And rush along, ten thousand strong,
To move, we know not whither.

While hundreds die along the way,
Our Exodus advances
Until we find some Promised Land
In which to take our chances.

Be not so near! Great God of Love,
So mating is less chronic,
And lemming life can be enriched
With friendships more platonic.

Thus we may learn to pass the days
In rest and conversation,
And live with more refined delights
And less of mass migration.

 FOOTNOTE — Warmly Dressed, Gregarious Mice

The lemming is a plump, warmly dressed, gregarious arctic animal related to the mouse. The most famous lemmings live in Scandinavia, where they have been extensively studied. They feed on tender roots and grass, and every two or three years a lemming population suddenly increases dramatically, forcing the whole camp to migrate in chaos in search of food. Many die in the frantic search.

Praxis for Today:

Follow the Few

"Animals are nothing but the forms of our virtues and vices wandering before our eyes," said Victor Hugo almost 200 years ago. "They are the visible phantoms of our own soul."

Thus, lemmings are, of course, famous metaphors for humans who follow the crowd, doing what is customary, habitual and popular. So today, as a spiritual exploration, do the exact opposite. Pick up the book that looks uninteresting. Fight against the compulsion to be busy. Try the unpopular brand, try the exotic food, listen to the offbeat radio station, read the magazine you despise. Look on someone you dislike with new, non-judgmental eyes.

As our lamenting lemming testifies, it is often just too much of a good thing that limits our life. Humans too are bundles of energy, powerpacks of good impulses that are hard to control. In our panic to make decisions, we often go along with the crowd — it is so much simpler than living mindfully, figuring out what is best.

So experiment with contrariness. Dream a new dream.

When something becomes the thing everyone wants to do, do the opposite. Today, for one day, follow the few: Live counterclockwise. Do something you normally never do. See if the new perspective brings enlightening experiences.

Millions have bought the book *The Road Less Traveled*. That proves a human instinct to sometimes avoid the common path. Try a road less traveled today.

Honest differences are often a healthy sign of progress.

—**Mahatma Gandhi**

Afterword
How the Tame Things Pray

Now that you know how the Wild Things pray, how about us "tame things"? How do we pray?

Of course, sometimes we pray like the Wild Things do in this book. We speak to God in words, words we get from a book or words we make up ourselves: requests, alleluias, thanks, praise. As for myself, I find that lately I easily fall silent before God. I've run out of words. Is this a kind of seasonal development on my spiritual path? Or have I risen at last into the stratospheric "prayer of simplicity" John of the Cross speaks of?

Silencing Your Voice: Using Mantras

When I was a young boy, I filled my missal with prayer cards. I would turn over the cards and read the prayers, speaking them to God or to the saints. My mother instructed me early in life to "pray as if you mean every word," so it might be authentic prayer. As I became more seasoned, of course, I made up my own prayers.

But now I am in a season of silence, or almost silence. I can easily imagine how a wolf or a salmon or a crab or a booby prays, but I find it hard to use words myself. As a substitute, I have come to like to repeat certain Latin words that are full of meaning for me (I grew up when the Mass was in Latin): *Veni* (Come), *Gratias* (Thanks), *Aspice* (Look). This last "mantra" is perhaps my favorite and is taken from Psalm 139: "Behold, O Lord, and look down on the face of your Christ" — which feels like being in solidarity with all the world's efforts to heal and grow.

At times I even hum the comforting mantra "ommm," thinking of it as suggesting the primitive utterance of a nursing infant. That sound is, appropriately enough, the very name of God for many Hindus, a sacred sound. Imagine! If the Hindus are right, the best name for God may be a sound taken from the lips of infants. (And note: The word infant means, "One who can't speak." That's just the way we may ultimately find ourselves before God.)

Many times, I simply remain silent in God's presence. Upon reflection, this also seems to make excellent sense. After all, although God speaks constantly and eloquently in creation and in our life, S/he seems to maintain a definite kind of silence: word-silence — at least according to most peoples' experience. Most of us do not hear God speaking to us in words. Were God to actually do so, we might feel obliged to reply in words, but this is not usually the case. So, once again, word-silence seems appropriate — at least sometimes.

At other times, words help us pray. Karl Rahner said that "to be religious" is "to believe that it is meaningful for a human being to speak into the endless desert of God's silence."

Yet isn't it true that, after all, it is our heart that prays our most true feelings and desires? Regardless of the words we put on our lips, God reads our hearts. Our task in prayer is always communion with God, not eloquent-sounding words.

In this light, there are lots of other ways theology teaches us to pray without words:

- accept your lot in life with largeheartedness
- preserve solidarity with the oppressed
- listen compassionately to the groans of those in pain
- love widely
- work hard
- share what you have
- enjoy life deeply and freely

God takes all such human actions — and many others — as ways of being "in communion with the Divine Heart," that is, as prayers.

To pray in this wordless way requires only a flick of perspective, yet everything can be suddenly different. The actions on this list are, in the presence of faith, the great prayers of the world. Why? In our formal church prayers and recited prayers, we are only imitating these most genuine acts of human caring. God reads it in our hearts. This point of view creates for us something like a stained-glass window looking out at the world. Out that window one can see the edifying reality of heavily burdened and patient people as "walking prayers," powerful forces for good in the world. They pray wonderfully without words.

Silencing Your Heart

At the crisis point in the biblical story of Job, the poor, overwhelmed fellow covers his mouth. He knew that he rightly should say nothing at all, just keep silence — in response to God's challenge to him when he did complain.

But we can take this further. Job's self-quieting, mouth-covering gesture would have been less than human if he did not at the same time quiet and silence his heart. Job silenced himself not to form an unfeeling heart of stone but to develop a heart acceptant of, familiar with and consonant with the mysteries of life. Such silence is a surrendering to an unknown and unknowable — but trustworthy — Reality, poised in readiness to endure the battering of fate and the cyclone winds of whatever unfathomable evils may come. This silent Job is a model for us all. It is the "fasting of the heart" of which Thomas Merton spoke. In this fasting we are willing to get along without answers to everything.

Sometimes the sheer awesomeness of God in created things also suggests silence: the mind-blowing design of DNA, the horrifying forces of hurricanes and earthquakes, the predatory wildness of animals, the dizzying speeds and distances in space, the astonishing beauty of our children, the disorienting anguish of illness. Thoughtful people may be driven to silence by these wonders — silence before God, that otherworldly Force and Personage we are unable even to name but whom, in theologian Elizabeth Johnson's phrase, we can only "name toward." We can name toward God, point to God, look to God, speechlessly. Not a bad prayer. "Wonder is at the heart of contemplation," said Anthony de Mello, and the greatest wonders invariably render us speechless.

After all, we are not, strictly speaking, ever obliged to pray. We need not feel guilt about such silence. Remember, God does not speak directly to us in words either. Rather, praying is a richness in life, a skill we will be wise to learn and practice because life itself invites us to it, even if we do it silently.

The Heart in Port

The poet Emily Dickinson says: "Joy delights in joy. Futile the winds to a heart in port."

A heart in port — like a ship in safe harbor — that's possibly the praying person's ideal. The aim of prayerfulness is reaching a place of spiritual poise beyond awe, even beyond despair — for many situations in our world are indeed hopelessly askew — yet the clock is always ticking, and, therefore, God is always still there to promise us a fulfilling future.

How can we get ready for a good silent prayer? By bringing together a mind widely aware and honest, and a heart in awe of the beautiful and good and in surrender to all the ultimates beyond one's self, a heart courageous in choosing life and everything vitalizing and worthy. Finally, I find it a big help to prayer when I can achieve "a light heart," willing to laugh at an alligator afraid of ducklings and goldfish, an eel with low self-esteem, a fox who wants to be trusted in the hen house, or a human who wants to write a whole book about prayer when he doesn't really know how to do it himself.

William Cleary

bcleary412@aol.com
http://members.aol.com/bcleary412

Spring 1999

Index